Flower Arrangement of Korea

Its Beauty and Spirit

Flower Arrangement

of Korea   *Its Beauty and Spirit*

by Chung Sun-ai

HOLLYM INTERNATIONAL CORP.
Elizabeth, New Jersey   Seoul

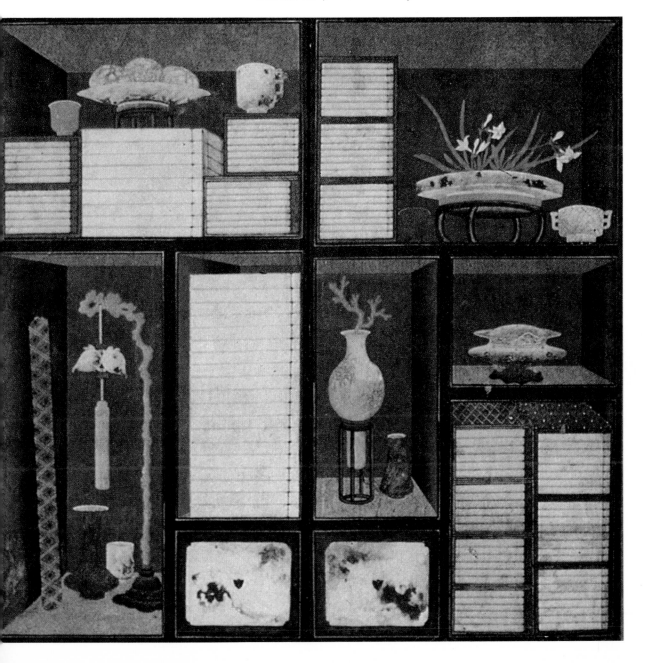

First published in 1984
Fourth printing, 1994
by Hollym International Corp.
18 Donald Place
Elizabeth, New Jersey 07208 U.S.A.
Phone: (908)353-1655   Fax: (908)353-0255

Published simultaneously in Korea
by Hollym Corporation; Publishers
14-5 Kwanchol-dong, Chongno-gu, Seoul 110-111, Korea
Phone: (02)735-7544   Fax: (02)730-5149

ISBN: 0-930878-36-1
Library of Congress Catalog Card Number: 84-80496

Printed in Korea

PREFACE

The flower does not boast of its beauty or envy the beauty of others, but simply sits there for the universe to admire, and it is the emblem of virtue and symbol of love.

Man's admiration of flowers led him in the desire to adorn his home with arranged flowers, and the art of flower arrangement developed in the East and the West according to feelings and nature.

Korean flower arrangement originated from Eastern part of the world. It is different from the Western style, which emphasizes harmony of color, form and quality. In Korean flower arrangement, space is left between flowers so that the flowers and space can create harmonious lines in its simplicity.

Flowers have a history, philosophy and certain principles of their own to be observed in their arrangements. Korean flowers have characteristics that have developed with the tradition, custom and rites of the Korean people.

It was by accident that I came to teach the Korean art of flower arrangement to foreigners. I believe that teaching them this arrangement is a good way to help them understand Korea, its people and culture. Often I felt very inadequate without any basic book in English on flower arrangement. This book will introduce the history and the methods of Korean flower arrangements.

I have also attempted to teach dried flower arrangement with Oriental lines, since many foreigners with an interest in dried flowers have a mistaken notion that there is only a Western way to arrange them.

I would like to express my sincere appreciation to Mr. Rhimm, In-soo, the president of Hollym Corporation, and Mr. Chu, Shin-won, the Director of the company. My gratitude also goes to all others who gave me advice and other support without whose help this book would not have been possible.

머리말

꽃은 神이 人間에게 주신 고귀한 선물 중의 하나라 할 수 있는데, 그 꽃은 향기와 함께 아름다움의 상징으로 우주만물과 더불어 인간의 生活을 윤택하게 해 주었습니다.

아름다움을 추구하는 인간의 끝없는 마음은 꽃과 나무를 집 안에서 키우기를 원하게 되었고, 나아가 생활의 감정과 자연과의 하아모니를 위해 더욱 가까이에서 손수 재창조적인 아름다움을 만드는 꽃꽂이를 하게 되었읍니다.

동양 꽃꽂이에 그 바탕을 둔 한국 꽃꽂이는 색채, 형태, 질감의 조화를 두는 서구 꽃꽂이와는 달리 선과 공간, 뭉치의 조화에 근본을 두고 있읍니다. 이는 음양의 이치를 살린 동양철학적인 은은하고 깊은 뜻을 담은 것이기도 합니다.

우연한 기회에 외국인들에게 한국 꽃꽂이를 가르치게 되었을 때, 관심은 많지만 우리의 꽃꽂이에 대해 전혀 모르는 그들에게 소개할 자료가 없어 안타까왔읍니다. 그래서 그들의 이해를 돕기 위해 한국 꽃꽂이의 역사와 함께 아주 기본적인 작품을 소개하고자 이 책을 엮게 되었읍니다.

또한 말린 화재에 관심이 많은 외국인들에게 도움을 주고자 한국적인 표현으로 몇 작품을 실었읍니다.

꽃꽂이를 통하여 우리 나라의 풍습과 전통을 소개할 수 있고, 우정과 사랑을 아낌없이 나눌 수 있으리라 생각합니다.

이 책을 내도록 도와주신 한림출판사 임 인수 사장님과 주 신원 전무님, 또 수고하여 주신 여러분께 진정한 감사를 드립니다.

CONTENTS

차 례

Works of Flower Arrangement

꽃꽂이 작품집

Peace of World

Materials : Camellia, Pine branch, Pinus koraiensis, Curly willow, Palm leaves, Chestnut branch, Bittersweet red rose, White rose, Violet chrysanthemum, Currant
Container : Old tree
Form : Free style

Several materials were put together to show good harmony. In this arrangement I tried to express the whole world living peacefully.

세계 평화

화 재 : 동백, 소나무, 잣나무, 곱슬버들, 종려잎, 밤나무, 빨간 장미, 흰 장미, 보라 중국, 까치밥
화 기 : 고목
화 형 : 자유형

여러 가지의 화재를 서로 조화 있게 처리한 작품으로, 세계의 모든 인류가 함께 평화스럽게 어울려 사는 것을 표현해 보았다.

□ The Morning of New Year

Materials : Bird of paradise, Camellia, Red rose, Pine branch
Container : Shilla period ceramic compote
Form : Upright free style

Method : One big and tall bird of paradise as the main line is arranged in an upright style. For the second line a pine branch is used to emphasize the line of the branch. The third line is formed with camellia and roses. Remove leaves from the roses and camellia before inserting.

Subordinate : First of all, cut the bird of paradise in two different lengths, and place them at the front and the back of the container. For the second line, the pine branch is trimmed and put toward the front. The third line is the camellias cut shorter than the regular third line length, leaving only few leaves. The rose is another third subordinate branch. The rose stems are cut short, again using only a few leaves. Cut the roses in water and insert them toward the front in an upright style. To enjoy the beauty of this arrangement for a long time, put a few drops of salt water in the camellia buds to prevent the blossoms from falling.

Comments : The bird of paradise expresses bright sunshine and the green pine branches show the will of our ancestors. Camellias and roses emphasize the red color.

□ 새해 아침

화　재 : 극락조, 동백, 빨간 장미, 소나무
화　기 : 신라 토기
화　형 : 바로세우는 자유형

꽃는 법 : 제1주지는 극락조로 똑바로 세워 꽂았다.
제2주지인 소나무는 선을 살리기 위해 가지를 다듬어 꽂았다.
제3주지는 동백꽃과 장미로 꽂는데 잎이 크므로 몇 개만 남기고 떼어낸 다음 꽂는다.

종지 넣기 : 극락조 2송이를 길이가 다르게 잘라 1주지를 꽂아 중심을 살려 준다. 제2주지는 앞쪽으로 소나무를 다듬어 2주지 종지로 꽂고, 동백꽃을 몇 개의 잎만 남겨 3주지와 같은 방향으로 3주지보다 짧게 하여 꽂아 준다.

역시 장미꽃은 제3주지의 종지로 길이를 짧게 하여 잎을 쳐낸 다음 물속자르기를 하여 앞을 향해 바로세워 꽂는다. 이 때 동백봉오리 속에 소금물을 주입시켜 낙화하는 것을 방지하도록 해 준다.

해　설 : 밝은 햇살을 닮은 황금색의 극락조로 새해 아침의 분위기를 살려 보았다. 옛 선조들의 꿋꿋한 의지를 담은 소나무로 한껏 푸르름을 강조시켜 붉은 동백과 장미를 돋보이게 하였다.

□ A Stubborn Person

Materials : Chinese plum branch, Salem, Aspidistra elatior, Yellow rose
Container : Shilla period ceramic compote
Form : Upright free style

Method : At first use a plum branch as the first line in an upright style. Choose plum branches that are not curved. The length of the branch is twice the vase length. The small twigs at the bottom of the branches must be trimmed. The second line is the aspidistra elatior leaf forming the soft line. Curve the leaves in your hand bending to make a graceful line. The third line is the salem and the roses. Cut the salem leaves short to get the overall balance. To prolong the freshness of the roses, place the stems in boiling salted water or burn the cut ends.

Subordinate : As the subordinate of first line, cut Chinese plum branch to one-third the length of the first main branch and insert it at the left side. Four or five leaves of orchids are inserted around the second main line as if coming from one branch. Yellow roses are the subordinates of the third main line. The tips of the rose stems are treated by burning. The length should be very short or two-thirds of the third main line.

Comments : The loftiness and straightforwardness of the plum tree in the snow depict the characteristics of the Korean people, and the harmony between the East and the West is reflected in this arrangement.

① ② ③

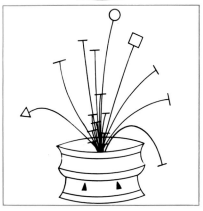

□ 고집장이

화　재：홍매화, 셀램, 잎난초, 노랑 장미
화　기：신라 토기
화　형：바로세우는 자유형

꽂는 법 : 제1주지는 홍매화 곧은 가지를 골라 그릇의 2배 정도로 길게 하여 꽂아 준다. 밑부분의 잔가지는 다듬어 주는 것이 좋다.
　제2주지는 잎난의 부드러운 선을 살려 오른쪽에 꽂는다. 곧은 잎은 손바닥에 놓고 훑으면 부드러운 곡선을 만들 수 있다.
　제3주지는 장미와 더불어 셀렘잎을 꽂는데 면이 넓으므로 짧게 잘라 다른 주지보다 크게 보이지 않도록 꽂는다.
종지 넣기 : 제1주지의 종지로 매화를 1주지 길이의 1/3 정도로 하여 1주지 왼쪽으로 꽂고, 4~5장의 잎난초는 2주지를 중심으로 한뿌리에 나온 것처럼 밑부분을 거의 붙이다시피 꽂고 자연스럽게 곡선을 만든다. 제3주지의 종지로 노랑 장미꽃을 줄기끝을 태워 꽂고, 아주 짧은 것에서부터 3주지의 2/3정도의 길이까지 다양하게 잘라 앞과 위를 향해 점층적으로 꽂아 마무리한다.
해　설 : 눈 속에서도 고고하게 피어나는 매화는 고집스러울 정도인 한국인의 곧은 마음과 청결함을 상징해 주었다. 서양인의 자연스러움을 닮은 셀렘잎과 잎난의 푸르름 사이에 장미꽃을 꽂아 단아한 매화를 더욱 곧게 보이도록 하였다.

☐ We Meet Again

Materials : Rhododendron, Branch of Korean pine, Orchid leaf, White middle chrysanthemum
Container : Korean kimchi jar cover
Form : Separated style

Method : The first line, rhododendron, is inserted straight on the left side of the pin-holder using only few leaves. The second line which is also rhododendron, cut one-half the length of the first line is put on the right side of it, using a few leaves. The third line, rhododendron, is inserted beside the first line at 80°

Subordinate : Insert orchid leaves, putting them together in a bunch and curving them with wire before inserting them between first and third lines and beside the second. Branches of the pine are used to give variety to the simpleness of the rhododendron. The chrysanthemums are used with a few leaves. Put the cut stems of the chrysanthemum in boiling salted water to retain freshness. And then insert them between the first and third lines.

Comments : A rustic kimchi jar cover makes an appropriate flower bowl, giving an Oriental atmosphere. By putting some small pebbles or shells between the first and second lines, you will get the feeling of whispering happiness, and by placing the orchid leaves face to face, the joy of meeting again.

☐ 다시 만남

화 재 : 영산홍, 잣나무 가지, 난잎, 흰 중국.
화 기 : 항아리 뚜껑
화 형 : 분리형(나누어꽂기)

꽂는 법 : 제 1주지는 왼쪽 침봉에 몇 개의 잎만 남겨 선을 살린 영산홍을 거의 똑바로 꽂는다.
　제 2주지는 영산홍을 오른쪽 침봉에 역시 몇 개의 잎만 남긴 1주지의 1/2정도의 길이로 꽂는다.
　제 3주지는 1주지 옆쪽으로 80° 정도 기울여 영산홍을 꽂아 준다.
종지 넣기 : 난잎을 묶어 손으로 곡선을 만든 다음 1주지와 3주지 사이, 그리고 2주지 옆에 꽂는다.
　영산홍가지의 단순함을 잣나무 가지를 꽂아 없애 주고, 국화는 잎을 다듬어 염열탕을 하여 1, 3주지 사이에 소담스럽게 꽂는다.
해 설 : 소박스러운 항아리 뚜껑을 화기로 하여 동양스러움을 물씬 풍겨 주었다.
　1주지와 2주지 사이에 잔 자갈이나 조개껍질을 깔아 마치 아기자기한 밀어들이 깔려진 듯하다. 난잎을 서로 마주 보게 하여 다시 만난 기쁨의 정을 나누는 모습을 표현해 주었다.

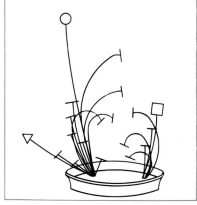

□ Up and Down

Materials : Chaenomeles, Pot marigold
Container : Subok porcelain bowl
Form : Free style

Method : Insert chaenomeles as the first line. Omit the second line and use marigolds as the third line. Marigolds are cut in the water and put at the right side of the container to make space.

Subordinate : The chaenomeles is three-fourths the length of the first line and is inserted at the left of the first line. Trim the leaves and flowers of the marigolds and insert the marigolds short in contrast to the chaenomeles.

Comments : Height is as endless as depth is bottomless. When could they ever meet? In this arrangement I emphasized the high and the low. We have an old saying that pot marigolds are named after a gold cup. The flower connotation is not a pleasant one; so one should avoid pot marigolds for an occasion of celebration.

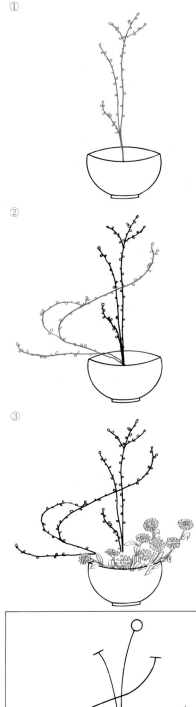

① ② ③

□ 上과 下

화　재 : 산당화, 금잔화
화　기 : 수복 도자기
화　형 : 자유형

꽂는 법 : 제 1주지는 산당화로 곧게 꽂고 제 2주지는 생략하여 1주지를 강조시켰다.

제 3주지는 금잔화를 물속자르기로 짧게 잘라 오른쪽에 꽂아 1주지와 공간을 두드러지게 하였다.

종지 넣기 : 산당화의 길이를 1주지의 3/4정도 길이로 하여 1주지 외쪽으로 꽂고, 금잔화는 잎과 꽃봉오리를 다듬어 산당화와는 대조적으로 짧게 앞을 향해 꽂는다.

해　설 : 끝없이 높고 한없이 낮음의 만남을 위해 꽂아 보았다. 살아가는 이치는 높고 낮음의 조화를 아름답도록 꾸며 보는 것이리라.

단 금잔화는 경사스러운 일에는 화재로 하는 것을 금하기로 한다.

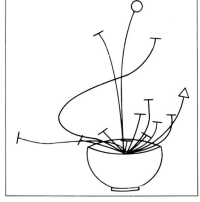

□ An Elegant Lady

Materials : Hedera helix, Yellow middle chrysanthemum
Container : Haegang's celadon vase
Form : Upright free style

Method : Hedera helix, which is a kind of ivy, is used as the first line, trimming the stem to make the form. Hedera helix are used as the second and the third lines. The branches with their soft lines are inserted erect to give a feeling of beautiful space. The third line is put opposite the second line.

Subordinate : Arrange trimmed chrysanthemums in the center between the first and third lines to create harmony with the straight branches:

Comments : One feels the typical Oriental wife (woman) of elegance. The blue beautiful lines of the celadon vase and the yellow chrysanthemums are harmonious.

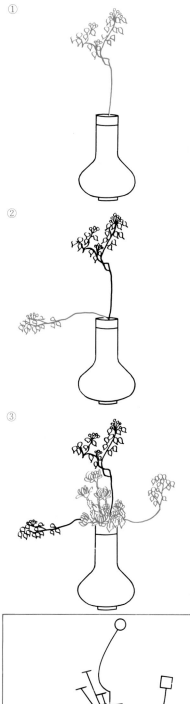

① ② ③

□ 귀부인

　화　재 : 금송악 (섬담쟁이), 황 중국
　화　기 : 해강의 청자
　화　형 : 바로세우는 자유형

　꽃는 법 : 제 1 주지는 섬담쟁이라는 담쟁이과에 속하는 나무로 거친 섬담쟁이를 뿌리와 선을 다듬어 꽂는다.
　제 2 주지 역시 금송악을 다듬어 곧은 가지의 1 주지와 어울리게 선이 부드러운 가지를 골라 꽂는다. 그렇게 하면 1 주지와의 공간이 훨씬 아름답다.
　제 3 주지는 거의 1 주지와 수직을 이루게 하여 2 주지 반대쪽에 꽂는다.
　종지 넣기 : 노란색 국화를 잎을 다듬어, 중앙에서 1 주지와 3 주지 사이의 공간을 향해 꽂아 선반으로 이루어진 딱딱함을 없애 주면서 앞과 위를 향해 꽂는다.
　해　설 : 고전적인 동양 여인의 우아한 느낌을 준다. 금송악을 곧게 세워 더욱 고고한 모습을 연출해 보았다.
　푸르름이 감도는 청자의 아름다운 선과 노란 국화의 조화가 곱다.

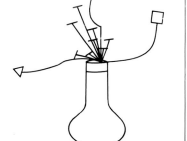

□ A Fireside Chat at Night

Materials : Common box tree, Gerbera, White freesia
Container : Brass fire pot (brazier)
Form : Slanting style

Method : Insert common box tree as the first line in a slanting style. The second and the third lines are put according to the form of the slant (about 10°).

Subordinate : Place red gerberas centering around the second line in an upright style like a flaming fire. Cut the white freesia in the water and put them lower than gerberas to emphasize the red color of the gerbera.

Comments : During the cold, long winter nights, people like to sit around the warm brazier such as this ancient Korean charcoal brazier, chatting, listening to old tales and eating roasted chestnuts. The brass brazier adds feeling of grandmother's touches.

①

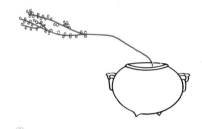

②

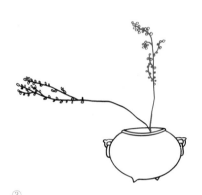

③

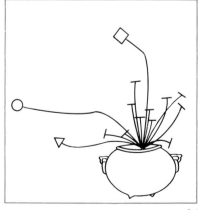

□ 노변야화 (爐辺夜話)

화　재 : 참회양목, 가베라, 흰 프리지아
화　기 : 놋화로
화　형 : 기울이는 형

꽂는 법 : 제1주지는 참회양목을 다듬어 기울여 꽂는다.
제2주지는 역시 참회양목으로 10° 정도 기울여 꽂는다.
제3주지도 참회양목을 기울여 꽂는다.

종지 넣기 : 붉은 가베라는 타오르는 불처럼 2주지를 중심으로 하여 곧게 꽂으며 3주지와 연결시켜 준다.
흰 프리지아는 물속자르기를 하여 가베라 밑으로 꽂아 가베라의 붉은빛을 강조시킨다.

해　설 : 한겨울 따뜻한 화롯가에 앉아 군밤을 구워 먹으며 듣는 먼 옛날이야기는 새록새록 정이 생겨난다.
작은 송이의 프리지아는 아기자기한 이야기를 쏟아 놓는 듯하고 깨끗이 닦은 놋화로는 인자하셨던 할머니의 손길을 느끼게 한다

☐ Camellia Lady

Materials : Camellia, Lily, Korean pine
Container : White porcelain vase
Form : Upright free style

Method : First, among the camellias, choose an appropriate one as the first main line and arrange it, taking off the leaves so that the line of the branch is visible. Use camellias as the first, second and third lines, leaving ample space between first and third lines.

Subordinate: Lilies are used as subordinate of the camellias and pines to support the lilies.

Comments : A virgin from the Southern Island is a symbol of purity. The white color of the porcelain and the line of the camellias make good harmony. Camellias flourish in Cheju Island in Korea, and popular songs and even hair oils are named after this beautiful flower.

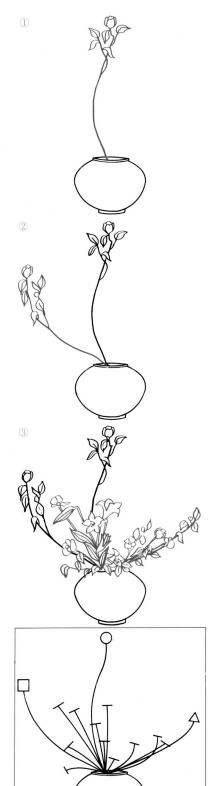

☐ 동백아가씨

화 재 : 동백, 백합, 잣솔
화 기 : 백자 항아리
화 형 : 바로세우는 자유형

꽃는 법 : 동백의 잎을 잘 다듬어 선을 살린 다음 제 1, 2, 3 주지를 선택하여 꽃는다.

제 1주지와 3주지 사이의 공간을 넉넉하게 두어 선을 최대한으로 살려 준다.

종지 넣기 : 백합을 1주지의 종지로 꽃고 잣나무 가지로 백합 주위를 보충시킨다.

해 설 : 남쪽 나라 어느 섬에서 봄을 기다리며 활짝 웃음을 머금은 처녀.

청순하고 싱그런 자태가 언제 보아도 사랑스럽다. 백항아리의 색깔과 선이 동백의 선과 싱싱하게 어우러지는 것이 특징이다.

한국에서는 제주도의 동백을 찬양한 노래와 동백기름이 유명하다.

☐ **Butterfly**

Materials : Azalea blossom
Container : Round vase
Form : Slanting free style

Method : In this slanting style use only the first and third lines, omitting the second line. Trim the azaleas boldly to make a good line of the branch.

Subordinate : In the center insert flowers in a bunch without branches. Azalea is good for a study of lines and also can be used alone without combining with other flowers.

Comments : Butterflies can go anywhere, flying and dancing with lovely wings. Butterflies! You cannot forget fragrance when thinking of the azaleas.

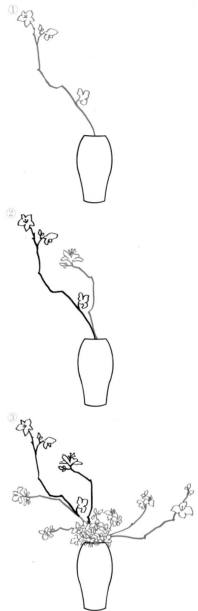

☐ 나 비

화 재 : 철쭉꽃
화 기 : 원형병
화 형 : 기울이는 자유형

꽃는 법 : 제 2 주지는 생략한 형으로 경사형으로 꽃는다. 제 1 주지 는 선을 살리기 위해 몇 송이만 남기고 과감하게 잘라낸다.
제 3 주지 역시 선을 살려 다듬어 꽃는다.

종지 넣기 : 같은 소재로 1주지와 3주지 사이에는 꽃만 뭉쳐서 주지의 선을 돋보이게 한다. 철쭉꽃은 선을 연습할 수 있는 재료이 며, 다른 소재와 배합이 없이도 꽃을 수 있다.

해 설 : 자유로이 그 가벼운 날개로.하늘하늘 춤을 추며 갈 수 있 는 나비. 나비야! 너는 철쭉의 향내를 못 잊어 하는구나.
화사한 봄날 철쭉 향내를 그리며 날아가는 나비를 표현해 꽃았다.

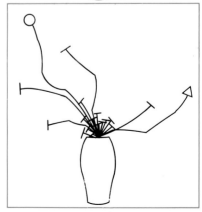

□ Three Sisters

Materials : New Zealand flax, White iris, Dracaena
Container : White porcelain bowl with patterns
Form : Upright free style

Method : Insert long white iris as the first line in an upright style. New Zealand flax is added to give strength to the flow of the line. The second line is omitted, and the third line is also the New Zealand flax to give volume.
Subordinate : Curve the leaves of the New Zealand flax before inserting to emphasize first line and bind with wire the dracaena in a little bunch.
Comments : We three sisters are always friendly and grateful to our parents, and I have tried to express that beautiful feeling of gratitude in this arrangement.

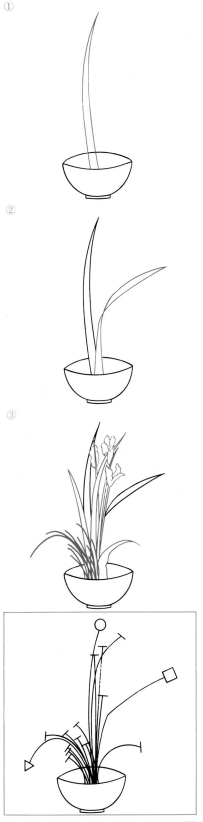

□ 세 자매

화　재 : 잎새란, 흰 아이리스, 드라세나
화　기 : 무늬 백자 수반
화　형 : 바로세우는 자유형

꽂는 법 : 제1주지로 흰 아이리스를 곧게 꽂는다.
제2주지는 잎새란을 자연스럽게 구부려 꽂아 준다.
제3주지도 잎새란의 선을 살려 꽂는다.
종지 넣기 : 1주지의 선을 잎새란을 넣어 흐름을 강하게 표시하고, 드라세나를 묶어 선을 구부린 다음 볼륨 있게 꽂아 동양적인 미를 살린다.
해　설 : 우애 깊은 세 자매, 부모님 사랑에 늘 감사하며 맑고 곧게 씩씩하게 자라는 모습을 난의 배합으로 표현해 보았다.

☐ **Marriage**

Materials : Sweet pea, Asparagus, Trumpet daffodil, Freesia, Orchid leaf

Container : A lamp-oil container

Form : Free style

Method : Use sweet pea as the first main line and asparagus as the second line. A bent flower signifies a shy bride. Orchid leaves are used as the third main line along with freesia.

Subordinate : In the middle of this frame daffodil is inserted in a bunch. Yellow, red and blue depict the bright colors of the multicolored Korean bridal costume. This lamp-oil container is made out of a log.

Comments : In the olden days, after a Korean wedding ceremony the bride waited for the groom under the dim light of the oil lamp. The bride in her colorful wedding dress wore heavy ornaments on her head, and the bridegroom had to remove all the ornaments before retiring.

①

②

③

☐ 결 혼

화 재 : 스위트피, 아스파라거스, 나팔수선, 프리지아, 난잎

화 기 : 등잔

화 형 : 자유형

꽂는 법 : 제 1주지는 스위트피로 꽂고, 제 2주지는 선이 고운 아스파라거스를 택하여 꽂는다.
제 3주지는 난잎을 프리지아와 곁들여 꽂았다.

종지 넣기 : 제 1주지는 주지를 푸른 아스파라거스로 꽂아 스위트피의 수줍은 모습을 살려 주고, 가운데 부분은 뭉치법으로 나팔수선을 꽂아 노랑, 빨강, 파랑으로 화려한 신부의 모습을 표현해 주었다.

해 설 : 한국의 오래된 전통적인 결혼 의식을 나타낸 작품. 등잔불 밑에 소곳이 앉아 신랑을 기다리는 신부의 모습이다. 무거운 족두리를 얹고 오색찬란한 신부복으로 성장한 신부는 신랑이 와야 쉴 수 있는 한국의 결혼 풍습을 표현해 보았다.

□ A Virgin in Spring

Materials : Curled willow, Yellow iris, White freesia, Orchis rupestris

Container : Kim, Ik-yong's ceramic compote

Form : Upright free style

Method : Insert the weeping willow straight up as the first line; for the second line, use the iris slightly slanting toward the first line. Cut off unnecessary leaves and insert them beside the flowers. Then insert freesia as the third line after binding the flowers with wire and cutting off the leaves.

Subordinate : Insert orchis rupestris between the flowers to emphasize the freshness of spring.

Comments : Spring is heralded by the first bud of the weeping willow. The materials used here make an appropriate spring flower arrangement with the old dead tree accenting the contrast with the fresh flowers.

□ 봄처녀

화　재 : 곱슬버들, 노란 아이리스, 흰 프리지아, 나비난초

화　기 : 도기 (김익영 작품)

화　형 : 바로세우는 자유형

꽃는 법 : 제1주지는 지저분한 선을 처리한 곱슬버들을 곧게 꽂는다.

제2주지는 아이리스로 약간 경사지게 꽂되 잎을 정리하여 꽂는다.
제3주지인 프리지아는 선을 살려 잎을 따내고 봉오리는 철사로 묶어서 사용한다.

종지 넣기 : 나비난초잎을 사이사이에 꽂아 봄의 신선함을 나타내주었다.

해　설 : 봄 소식을 전하는 곱슬버들의 자연스러운 선을 살린 작품으로 고목을 곁들여 더욱 고풍스러운 멋과 함께 신선함을 강조하였다.

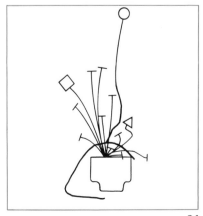

□ An Impromptu Fantasy

Materials : Trumpet daffodil, Anemone, Baby's breath
Container : Marble sculpture of a woman
Form : Free style

Method : Use the trumpet daffodil as the first line, cutting off any unnecessary leaves, and bending them one by one to the line, inserting them closely around the flowers as if coming out of one root. Apply the same method to the trumpet daffodils as the second line. The anemone is used as the third line.

Subordinate : Insert baby's breath between first, second and third lines to give contrast to the black container. When using baby's breath, bind them together to insert easily.

Comments : Anemone symbolizes the attitudes of a dancing princess. The black marble sculpture expresses beauty and mystery.

①

②

③

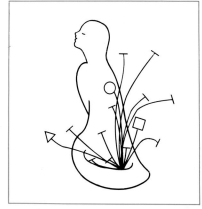

□ 즉흥 환상곡

화　재 : 나팔수선, 아네모네, 안개초
화　기 : 대리석 조각
화　형 : 자유형

꽃는 법 : 제 1 주지로 잎을 떼어 낸 나팔수선을 꽂고, 떼어 낸 잎은 손으로 선을 만들어 꽃과 같은 뿌리에서 나온 듯 꽂아 준다.
　제 2 주지 역시 나팔수선의 길이를 짧게 하여 곧게 꽂아 주는데, 1 주지와 마찬가지로 잎을 떼어 손질하여 꽂는다.
　제 3 주지는 아네모네로 옆으로 눕혀 꽂는다.
종지 넣기 : 제 1, 2 주지와 제 3 주지 사이에 안개초를 조금씩 묶어 꽂아 주고, 사이에 아네모네를 꽂아 화려한 느낌을 주도록 한다.
해　설 : 어느 왕비의 춤추는 모습을 상징한 아네모네의 신비스러움을 강조시킨 작품으로 수선잎을 좀더 강조시켜도 무방하다. 위의 작품을 검은 수반에 꽂아 더욱 신비하고 화려한 느낌을 준다.

☐ Ode to Autumn

Materials : Wild smilax, Cycad, White carnation
Container : Traditional Korean hat-shaped compote
Form : Slanting free style

Method : Use wild smilax as the first line and the second line. Insert them in a slightly slanting style. Heavy fruits are removed to make the line. Bend the branches to the direction you want. Use the white carnation as the third line.

Subordinate : Cycad is bent to a curved shape with a wire inside the leaf. The lines of the smilax and the curving leaves of the cycad make good harmony.

Comments : The smilax creates the perfect line for this autumn display. Like a walk in the woods, this arrangement gives you the feeling of freedom and brisk freshness of the fall season.

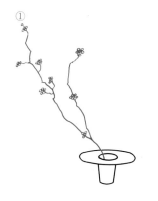

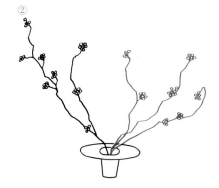

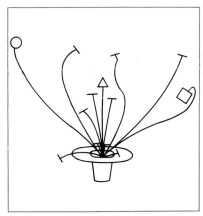

☐ 가을의 노래

화 재 : 망개나무, 소철, 흰 카네이션
화 기 : 갓 모양의 토기
화 형 : 기울이는 자유형

꽂는 법 : 제 1 주지와 2 주지는 망개로 꽂는데 무거운 열매와 잎을 떼어 내고 선을 만들어 약간씩 휘어서 기울이게 한다.
제 3 주지는 흰 카네이션을 곧게 꽂는다.

종지 넣기 : 소철은 철사를 사이에 넣어 구부린 다음 선을 다듬어 꽂는다. 선을 강조한 망개나무와 탐스런 소철의 잎을 조화시킨다.

해 설 : 가을 내음을 물씬 풍겨 주는 망개나무의 붉은 열매가 사랑스러움을 느끼게 한다.
숲 속을 거니는 것처럼 가을의 자유스러움과 신선함을 피부로 느끼게 하는 작품이다.

☐ Blue Sky

Materials : Winged spindle branch, Dry foxtail grass, Yellow lily

Container : White (ceramic) porcelain bowl

Form : Upright free style

Method : Insert winged spindle branch straight as first, second and third lines. You can bend the branches as you wish.

Subordinate : Dried materials are used high and low. Green leaves used in mass and the high yellow line make a colorful contrast.

Comments : The autumn sky is high and blue with the cool wind suggesting the harvest season.

① ② ③

☐푸른 하늘

화　재 : 화살나무, 말린 강아지풀, 황백합

화　기 : 백자기

화　형 : 바로세우는 자유형

꽂는 법 : 제 1, 2, 3 주지는 화살나무로 꽂는다. 비사실적인 꽃꽂이로 마음대로 꺾어 쓸 수 있는 것이 특징이다.

종지 넣기 : 마른 강아지풀을 위아래로 뭉쳐, 선과 뭉치의 조화를 시도하였다. 또한 마른 화재와 푸른색의 꽃을 함께 사용하여 색의 조화를 느끼게 하였다.

해　설 : 서늘한 바람이 스치는 가을 하늘은 높고 또 푸르다. 풍성한 추수의 계절이기도 하다.

□ Feeling

Materials : Elegant lily, Peperomia, Orchid leaf
Container : Korean stone basin from Cheju Island
Form : Free style

Method : Insert lily as the first line, orchid as the second line and peperomia as the third branch. Insert peperomia in a slanting style, contrasting with the orchid leaves.

Subordinate : Big-faced flowers are put in the center to form the focal point and they are cut shorter than the small-faced flowers. The peperomia leaves add to the roundness, and the orchid leaves, a curved line to the form.

Comments : If there is love, it will bloom in the shape of roundness and mist. No one can stop one's natural feelings. Here I tried to add a few delicate lines.

①

②

③

□ 감 정

화 재 : 빈틈나리, 페페로미아, 난잎
화 기 : 제주도 돌수반
화 형 : 자유형

꽂는 법 : 제 1주지는 빈틈나리로 곧게 꽂았다.

제 2주지는 난잎을 손으로 선을 만들어 자연스러운 모습으로 구부러지도록 한다.

제 3주지는 페페로미아를 옆으로 눕혀 난잎과 대조적인 강한 선을 조화시킨다.

종지 넣기 : 큰 꽃을 가운데 꽂아 포인트를 두고 작은 꽃의 얼굴은 위를 향해 꽂는다.

해 설 : 인간의 무수한 감정들을 연출해 본 꽃꽂이, 사랑이 있다면 둥글게 안개처럼 피어날 거예요. 감정의 흐름은 그 누구도 막을 수 없지요. 미묘한 선으로 살려 보았다.

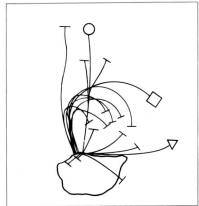

☐ Melody of Spring

Materials : Pine branch, Rape blossoms, White middle chrysanthemum
Container : Korean wood basket (a carrier's basket)
Form : Upright free style

Method : Put the pine branch as the first line and cut off some of the pine cones to form the line. Insert white middle chrysanthemums as the second line, using a few leaves. Insert rape blossoms as the third line.
Subordinate : Arrange different sizes of white chrysanthemums and rape blossoms around second line. Cut rape blossoms in the water twice. The freshness of the chrysanthemums is maintained by putting the tips of the stems in boiling salted water.
Comments : A bundle of flowers is put in the carrier's basket, and the line of the larch is beautiful as if dancing to the rhythm of a delightful melody.

①

②

③

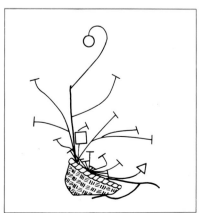

☐봄의 선율

화 재 : 낙엽송, 유채화, 흰 중국
화 기 : 삼태기
화 형 : 바로세우는 자유형

꽂는 법 : 제 1 주지는 솔방울을 대강 떼어 내고 다듬은 낙엽송으로 꽂는다.
제 2 주지는 흰 국화로 꽂고 잎을 약간 다듬어 준다.
제 3 주지는 유채화로 꽂는다.
종지 넣기 : 크기가 다른 흰 국화를 2 주지 둘레에 탐스럽게 꽂고 유채화를 곁들인다.
유채화는 물속자르기로 처리를 하고 국화는 염열탕으로 줄기 끝을 지지면 꽃이 오래 간다.
해 설 : 한없이 소박한 멋을 풍기는 삼태기 속에 푸짐한 꽃은 아름다운 선율을 따라 춤을 추듯 선이 곱다.

□ Poppy

Materials : Spiraea salicifolia, Poppy, Polygonatum falcatum

Container : Octagonal ceramic compote from Pyonsan

Form : Slanting free style

Method : Insert spiraea salicifolia branches in slanting style, forming the main first and second lines. The third line is the poppy, put in the center of the container, giving accent to the form. As the stem of the poppy is weak, use a fine wire through the stem or bind the wire and the stem together with tape.

Subordinate : The same materials as the main three branches are used, cutting them shorter than the main branches. Polygonatum falcatum is inserted on one side to give balance.

Comments : According to a Korean folk story, Yang Kwi-bi was the Queen of Hyunjong in the Tang Dynasty. The Queen was so beautiful that the flower was named after her. The poppy makes a colorful combination with polygonatum falcatum.

①

②

③

□ 양귀비

화　재 : 꼬리조팝나무, 양귀비, 진황정

화　기 : 변산의 8각 수반

화　형 : 기울이는 자유형

꽂는 법 : 제1주지와 제2주지는 조팝나무를 옆으로 뉘어서 꽂는다.

　제3주지는 양귀비로 약간 기울여 가운데 꽂는다. 양귀비는 대가 약하므로 철사나 테이프로 감아 꽂는 것이 좋다.

　종지 넣기 : 각기 다른 크기의 양귀비를 3주지와 같이 약간씩 기울여 가운데 꽂는다.

　진황정을 한쪽으로 꽂아 전체적으로 기울여 꽂은 것과 균형을 준다.

　해　설 : 중국 당나라 때 현종의 귀비로 그 美를 과시했던 양귀비를 닮아 그 이름이 붙었는지 알 수 없지만, 화려하고 아름다운 양귀비는 꼬리조팝나무와 어울려 더욱 화려해 보인다.

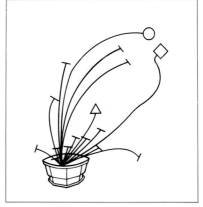

43

☐ First Daughter-in-law

Materials : Violet iris, Sansevieria, Dracaena
Container : Wooden container
Form : Upright style

Method : Insert iris as the first line after taking off the unnecessary leaves. The second line, sansevieria, emphasizes the broad line. Dracaena, the third line, is put in a bundle giving contrast to the line above and the volume below. Since sansevieria is very straight, curve the sansevieria by the twisting method before putting into the container.

Comments : This form emphasizes the upright style. The atmosphere of this arrangement reminds us of a virtuous daughter-in-law who is intelligent and mature.

① ② ③

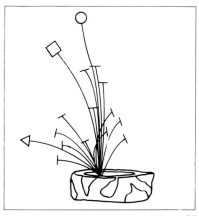

☐ 맏며느리

화　재 : 보라 아이리스, 산세비에리아, 드라세나
화　기 : 나무 수반
화　형 : 바로세우는 형

꽂는 법 : 제 1 주지는　잎을 간추린 아이리스로 곧게 꽂는다.
제 2 주지는 산세비에리아를 손으로 곡선을 만들어 꽂아 넓은 선을 강조시켜 준다.
제 3 주지는 드세라나를 뭉쳐서 꽂아 위의 선과 아래의 볼륨에 균형을 준다.
해　설 : 바로세우는 형의　전형적인 꽃꽂이이다. 어딘가 덕스럽고 지성적인 한국의 맏며느리를 연상케 하는 모습이다.

45

☐ East and West

Materials : Pear branch, Gladiolus, Dieffenbachia
Container : Traditional Korean jar
Form : Slanting free style

Method : For the first line use the pear branch in a slanting style. The second line is also the pear branch and gladiolus is the third. Take off leaves and top flowers of gladiolus and then cut the stems in the water to maintain freshness especially during hot weather.
Subordinate : Broad-leaved dieffenbachia are inserted in the middle, and gladiolus are put in a bundle with the green leaves. The flow of the lines is emphasized by this method.
Comments : I thought of the exchange of Korean and Western cultures and the friendship between different countries by arranging the pear(Eastern) and gladiolus (Western) together.

①

②
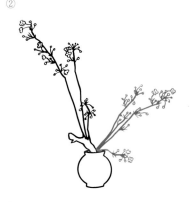

③

☐동과 서

화　재 : 배꽃, 글라디올러스, 디에펜밧키아
화　기 : 백항아리
화　형 : 기울이는 자유형

꽂는 법 : 제1주지로 배나무 가지를 다듬어 기울여 꽂는다.
제2주지도 배나무 가지로 꽂는다.
제3주지는 물속자르기한 글라디올러스를 잎과 꼭대기 꽃을 따내어 꽂는다.
종지 넣기 : 넓고 시원한 디에펜밧키아를 중앙에 꽂고 그 사이에 글라디올러스를 뭉쳐서 꽂아 선의 흐름을 더욱 강조한다.
해　설 : 동양적인 느낌의 배나무와 서양적인 글라디올러스를 배합하여 동서양의 우정을 그려 보았다.

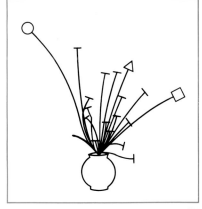

☐ A Dinner Party

Materials : White Chinese plum(Prunus mume), Calla lily, Angel carnation, Torreya tree
Container : Celadon vase
Form : Slanting free style

Method : Insert the plum branches as the first, second and third lines for the three main lines. Trim the branches to emphasize the shape.
Subordinate : Calla lily and angels are put crossing each other to give variety to the form. Angels are used as a bunch. Insert torreya branches to cover the base.
Comments : The attractiveness of plum blossoms reminds me of a peaceful dinner party Most Orientals love the plum tree and enjoy arranging its flowers. I arranged this with a feeling of thankfulness.

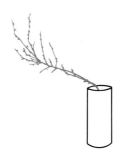

①

②

③

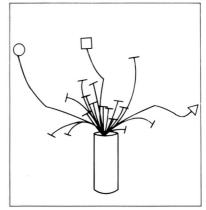

☐ 만찬회

화　재 : 옥매화, 칼라, 엔젤카네이션, 비자나무
화　기 : 자기병
화　형 : 기울이는 자유형

꽃 는 법 : 제 1, 2, 3, 주지는 옥매화가지를 다듬어 선을 살려 꽂는다.
종지 넣기 : 옥매화가지의 단조로움을 피하기 위해 물속자르기를 한 칼라의 얼굴을 서로 어긋나게 꽂는다.
엔젤카네이션은 꽃송이가 작으므로 뭉쳐 꽂는 것이 좋다. 비자나무를 밑받침용으로 사용하여 양감 있게 분위기를 살렸다.
해　설 : 앙징스럽도록 작은 옥매화 꽃송이는 화기애애한 미소 속에 맞는 만찬회같다.
보람된 하루의 감사와 내일에 대한 푸른 기대를 축복하는 마음으로 꽂아 본 작품이다.

☐ Children's Mind

Materials : Pussy willow, Sunflower, Calathea, White chrysanthemum
Container : Salad bowl
Form : Slanting free style

Method : Make curved lines with the pussy willow for the first line. Bend them with your fingers to make the form you desire. The first branch is placed in a little slanting style. Sunflowers are used as the second line with their faces crisscrossing. Insert calathea as the third line.
Subordinate : Put the chrysanthemums in the bottom to give a feeling of stability. Take off the leaves of the sunflowers as they wither fast and replace them with calathea leaves to add volume.
Comments : This arrangement with fresh sunflowers portrays the mind of a child that is always bright and green.

①

②

③

☐ 동 심

화　재 : 버들강아지, 해바라기, 칼라테아, 흰 국화
화　기 : 샐러드 그릇
화　형 : 기울이는 자유형

꽂는 법 : 제 1 주지는 버들강아지를 손으로 휘어서 원하는 선을 만들어 경사지게 꽂는다.
제 2 주지는 잎을 떼고 해바라기를 어긋나게 꽂는다.
제 3 주지는 칼라테아로 꽂는다.
종지 넣기 : 흰 국화를 제 3 주지를 중심으로 안정감을 주도록 꽂는다. 잎을 떼어 낸 해바라기 줄기는 칼라테아를 꽂아 볼륨 있게 보이도록 한다.
해　설 : 청초하고 푸르기만한 어린아이의 마음을 담은 작품으로 너무 활짝 피지 않은 해바라기가 오히려 싱싱하다.

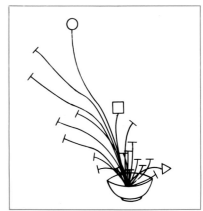

☐ Hula Dancing

Materials : Dogwood, Osmunda japonica, Small violet chrysanthemum
Container : A dish from Samoa Island
Form : Separated style

Method : First and third lines are arranged in separated forms and the second line is omitted. Insert the first line, dogwood, giving focal point to the line of the branch. For the third line, use osmunda japonica. The movement of osmunda japonica can be very interesting.
Subordinate : In the separated style it is important to make space between the first line and the third line. Insert small chrysanthemums between the first and the third branches.
Comments : While arranging these flowers in the dish from Samoa Island, I imagined young native girls of the Island dancing beautifully in their grass skirts.

②

③

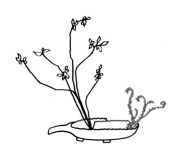

☐ 훌라 댄스

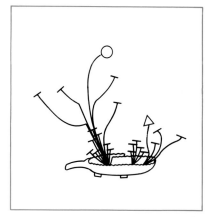

화 재 : 층층나무, 고비, 보라 소국
화 기 : 사모아의 접시
화 형 : 분리형

꽃는 법 : 제 2 주지를 생략한 형이다. 제 1 주지는 층층나무를 선을 살려 꽂는다.
제 3 주지는 고비의 율동이 깃든 듯한 선을 살려 꽂는다.
종지 넣기 : 제 1, 3 주지 주위를 작은 국화를 꽂아 전체적인 흐름을 이어 준다.
해 설 : 이국적인 사모아의 접시를 이용하여 꽂꽂이한 이 작품은 흥겨운 분위기를 준다.
섬 소녀가 치마를 흔들며 아름답게 춤을 추는 모습을 상상하여 표현해 보았다.

☐ The Ocean, Chorus of Shells

Materials : Cyclamen, Dracaena
Container : White square water basin
Form : Separated style

Method : The materials for the first and the second lines are cyclamen. For the third line, dracaenas are inserted as if they are coming out of the rocks.

Subordinate : You can also put small bundles of cyclamen around the third line.

Comments : The small rocks are picked from the seashore and are used to add variety. The mermaids are lifting up their heads to yearn for water. I arranged this one longing for the sea and trying to hear the songs of the shells in the swelling sea.

①

②

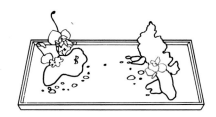

③

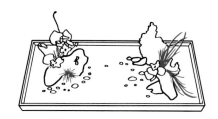

☐ 바닷가 조개들의 합창

화 재 : 시클라멘, 드라세나
화 기 : 흰 4각 수반
화 형 : 분리형

꽂는 법 : 돌밑에 침봉을 넣어 감추고 분리시켜 꽂는 형으로 제 1, 2주지는 시클라멘으로 꽂는다.
제 3주지는 드라세나를 조금씩 묶어 꽂는다.

종지 넣기 : 제 3주지 주위의 단순함을 피하기 위해 시클라멘을 곁들인다.

해 설 : 바닷가에서 주워온 작은 돌을 이용한 작품. 인어는 물이 그리워 고개를 든다. 물결 넘실거리는 바다 조개들의 노래 소리가 들리는 듯하다. 실내에서 바다를 그리며 꽂았다.

☐ Passion

Materials : Common aspidistra, Dahlia, Baby's breath, Cordyline
Container : White bowl
Form : Free style

Method : Choose common aspidistra as the first line. Make the desired line of the leaves by bending with your fingers and insert it in a position to appear as if coming out of one root of a plant. Insert dahlia as the third line.
Subordinate : Cordylines are shown between aspidistra, and white baby's breath is inserted between red dahlias.
Comments : The white container and red dahlias make good contrast, and the blue leaves of aspidistra look even more fresh.

①

②

③

☐ 열 정

화 재 : 잎난초, 다알리아, 안개초, 홍죽
화 기 : 흰 단지
화 형 : 자유형

꽂는 법 : 제 1주지는 손으로 선을 다듬은 잎난초를 꽂는다. 제 2주지도 잎난초로 꽂는데 마치 한뿌리에서 난 듯 꽂아 준다. 제 3주지는 다알리아로 꽂는다.
종지 넣기 : 잎난초 밑에 크지 않은 홍죽을 넣어 주고, 다알리아 사이사이에 안개초를 꽂아 다알리아의 색상을 살린다.
해 설 : 순백의 화기에 붉은 다알리아가 정열적으로 돋보인다. 시원스레 뻗은 잎난초가 더없이 싱싱하다.

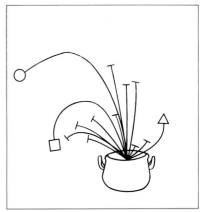

□ Song of Magnolia

Materials : Magnolia, Vine pear, Tulip, Cypress
Container : Lined ceramic bowl
Form : Upright style

Method : Cut magnolia branches boldly to make the desired line before using them as the first line. The second line is the vine pear held with wires. Choose the tulip as the third line and put a little sugar in the water to make the tulip last longer.

Subordinate : Cypress is inserted beside the first line.

Comments : I cannot help singing when the magnolias bloom. One can always remember the soft breezes of April in among the magnolias.

①

②

③

□ 목련의 노래

화　재 : 목련, 다래덩굴, 튜울립, 편백
화　기 : 줄무늬 자기
화　형 : 바로세우는 자유형

꽂는 법 : 제 1 주지는 목련의 선을 다듬어 꽂는다. 선을 정리할 때 대담하게 가지를 쳐 주는 것이 좋다.
제 2 주지는 다래덩굴을 다듬어 선을 살린 다음 철사로 묶어 꽂는다.
제 3 주지는 설탕을 주입시킨 튜울립으로 한다.
종지 넣기 : 제 1 주지 옆 부분의 공백을 없애기 위해 편백을 꽂았다.
해　설 : 목련이 피면 늘 생각나는 4 월의 노래. 당당함마저 깃든 목련의 우아함 속엔 부드러운 4 월의 미풍이 떠나질 않는 듯하다.

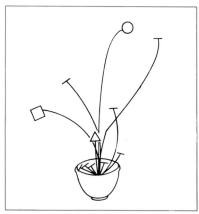

☐ Period of Royal Authority

Materials : Big pine branch, Colored kochia, Lily, Kalanchoe
Container : Shilla earthenware compote
Form : Upright free style

Method : Spread out the big pine branch and insert it straight as the first line. Use dried and dyed red kochia as the second line, moistened a little to make the forming of the desired line easy. Insert lilies as the third line.
Subordinate : Kalanchoes are used in a bundle to give balance to the form. Cut the stems of lilies and kalanchoes in water.
Comments : The big pine is the best among the pine trees. This tree can be compared to a mighty king who rules the whole country.

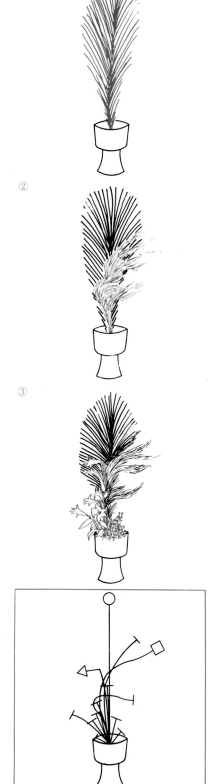

① ② ③

☐ 왕권시대

화　재 : 대왕솔, 착색한 댑싸리, 백합, 칼란코에
화　기 : 신라 토기
화　형 : 바로세우는 응용형

꽃는 법 : 제 1 주지는 곧게 뻗은 대왕솔을 택하여 꽂는다.
제 2 주지는 염색한 댑싸리를 물에 적셔 선을 만들어 꽂는다.
제 3 주지는 백합으로 꽂는다.
종지 넣기 : 단조로움을 피하기 위해 제 3 주지 옆에 칼란코에를 다복하게 꽂아 준다.
해　설 : 솔 중에 제일 좋은 대왕솔은 의젓한 품위를 지닌 어느 시대의 왕을 생각나게 한다.
백합과 칼란코에는 물속자르기를 하여 쓴다.

☐ **What Can I Do?**

Materials : Golden bell (forsythia), Pussy willow, Red carnation

Container : Modern ceramic water basin

Form : Slanting free style

Method : Choose golden bell as the first line. Curve the stem with hands little by little, to make the desired line and insert it in the basin. Place golden bell flowers low. With pussy willow as the second line, you can make any form of line you want. Insert carnation straight up as the third line.

Subordinate : Insert carnations short, and put them as a bundle.

Comments : This is an arrangement with spring flowers, expressing the ever-changing mood of spring with center of our mind remaining the same.

①

②

③

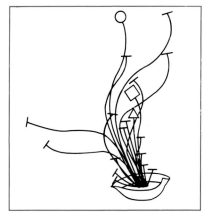

☐ 어떻게 할까 ?

화　재 : 개나리, 버들강아지, 빨간 카네이션
화　기 : 현대식 자기
화　형 : 기울이는 자유형

꽃는 법 : 제1주지는 개나리를 손으로 조금씩 휘어서 선을 만들어 꽃는다.
제2주지 역시 손으로 부드러운 선으로 다듬은 버들강아지로 꽃는다.
제3주지는 카네이션을 곧게 꽃는다.

종지 넣기 : 카네이션을 짧게 잘라 밑에 뭉치로 꽃는다.

해　설 : 봄철 화재를 주로 쓴 작품으로 금방 변하기 쉬운 마음을 표현하였다. 그래도 마음 한가운데에는 중심이 있는 것.

☐ Yudal Mountain

Materials : Big pine branch, Marguerite, Thistle, Spiraea
Container : Mountain sculpture
Form : Upright free style

Method : Insert the pine as the first line, spiraea as the second branch, and red thistle as the third line.

Subordinate : Marguerites are placed between red thistle and fixed in an oasis which is covered with moss.

Comments : Spring has come, but ice still remains here and there. Frogs are still sleeping even though flowers are blooming. I have tried to depict a mountain scene in early springtime.

☐ 유달산

화 재 : 대왕솔, 마아거리이트, 엉겅퀴, 조팝나무
화 기 : 유달산 모형조각
화 형 : 바로세우는 자유형

꽃는 법 : 제1주지는 대왕솔을 바로 세워 꽂는다.
제2주지는 조팝나무를 꽂는다.
제3주지는 붉은색 엉겅퀴로 꽂는다.

종지 넣기 : 오아시스를 고정시킨 뒤 땅밭으로 가려준다. 흰 마아거리이트를 엉겅퀴 사이에 꽂아 붉은색을 강조시킨다.

해 설 : 잔설이 남은 이른봄, 꽃은 피어도 개구리는 잠들고 있는 자연을 배경으로 꽂은 작품. 유달산이 조각되어진 돌을 화기로 삼아 꽂았다.

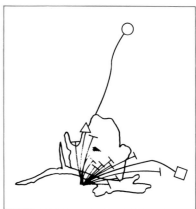

☐ Never-Changing Chunhyang

Materials : Pine branch, Curled willow, Yellow chrysanthemum

Container : Old tree roots

Form : Free style

Method : First choose the root of an old tree and fix it with wires. After placing an oasis in the root, insert curled willow, pines and chrysanthemums between them. Curled willow is the first line; pine branches the second and the third lines.

Subordinate : Chrysanthemums are inserted between the second and the third branches. The yellow color is emphasized.

Comments : In an ancient Korean folklore, Chunhyang and Yi, Mong-ryong love each other. With pine and chrysanthemum I tried to express Chunhyang's never changing love. In the garden the traditional Korean roof and chimney are shown.

①

②

③

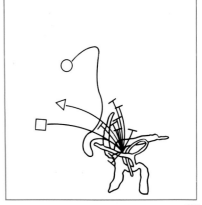

☐ 춘향이의 일편단심

화　재：소나무, 곱슬버들, 황국

화　기：오래된 나무 뿌리

화　형：자유형

꽂는 법：우선 고목 뿌리를 골라 철사로 고정시키고, 오아시스를 넣어 역시 고정시킨다.

곱슬버들을 제1주지로 하고, 제1주지와 같은 방향으로 제2주지인 소나무를 꽂는다.

제3주지는 소나무로 꽂는데 제1, 2주지와 같은 방향을 향해 꽂는다.

종지 넣기：소나무와 버들은 큰 선을 살려 그대로 꽂고 국화는 소나무의 앞뒤로 넣어 노랑색을 강조시켜 꽂는다.

해　설：우리 전설에 이 몽룡과 춘향이의 사랑 이야기는 유명하다. 절개와 사랑을 담은 춘향이의 변치 않는 마음을 소나무와 국화를 소재로 하여 고전적인 지붕이 있는 정원에 표현해 보았다.

□ Water Mill

Materials : Golden bell(forsythia), Bird of paradise, Pine branch, Kakuremino, Lily

Container : Kimchi jar

Form : Upright style

Method : Start with golden bell as the first line, bird of paradise flower and lilies as the second line, and pine branch as the third line.

Subordinate : Put kakuremino and lilies between the second line and the first line. Cover the empty space with curved pine branches.

Comments : A water mill goes around and around. . . . Sitting in an arbor, Koreans exchanged poems they wrote as they held their meetings.

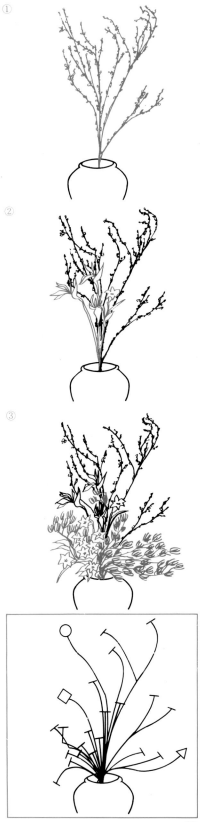

① ② ③

□물레방아

화 재 : 개나리, 극락조, 소나무, 황칠나무, 백합

화 기 : 김치독

화 형 : 바로세우는 형

꽃는 법 : 제 1 주지는 개나리를 정리하여 꽃는다.
제 2 주지는 선을 잘 다듬어 극락조와 백합을 꽃는다.
제 3 주지는 소나무를 선을 만들어 꽃는다.

종지 넣기 : 황칠나무와 백합을 제 2 주지 밑으로 꽂아 준다.
소나무는 면을 넓게 하여 특징을 살리는 것이 좋다.

해 설 : 돌고 도는 물레방아, 정자에 앉아서 시조를 읊으시던 옛 어른들, 여기가 모임의 장소이고 시를 교환하는 장소이었던 곳. 옛 스런 정을 표현해 보았다.

☐ Patience

Materials : Horsetail(scouring rush), Marguerite, Elegance carnation
Container : Rocks and root
Form : Free style

Method : Rocks and the root of an old tree are nature's containers. Place a pin-holder in the rock and hide it with moss. Horsetails, spread like arrows are the first line. Elegance is the second and marguerite is the third line.
Subordinate : Use the same materials as in the main branches, but cut them shorter than the main branches.
Comments : I wait, patiently resisting the temptation to break away and think. The green and slender horsetails and the old root make an interesting combination.

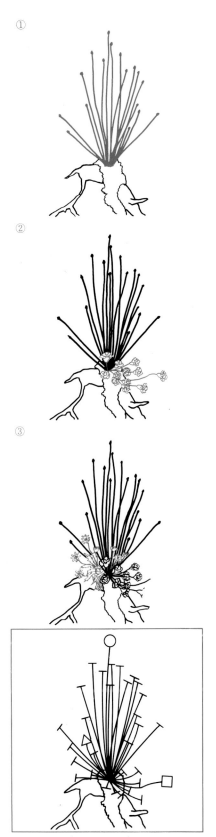

① ② ③

☐ 인 내

화 재 : 속새, 마아거리이트, 엘레강스카네이션
화 기 : 자연의 바위와 고목의 뿌리를 이용
화 형 : 자유형

꽂는 법 : 자연 그대로의 모양에 침봉을 넣고 풀잎으로 가려준 뒤 시작한다.
제 1 주지는 속새로 하는데 길이를 각기 다르게 하여 사방으로 퍼서 꽂는다.
제 2 주지는 엘레강스카네이션으로 꽂고, 제 3 주지는 마아거리이트로 꽂는다.
종지 넣기 : 1 주지의 종지는 속새로 키가 작게 꽂고, 2 주지는 작은 엘레강스카네이션을 사이에 꽂는다. 3 주지는 마아거리이트로 작게 꽂는다.
해 설 : 어디론가 뛰어나가고 싶은 욕망을 은은하게 삭히며 기다림을 배우는 모습을 닮았다.
푸른 속새와 고목의 색이 대조적이면서도 뭔가 진한 연결이 있어 보인다.

☐ **Harvest**

Materials : Colored silk grass, Dried oak tree, Indian millet, Ground cherry, Dried mugwort

Container : Korean carrier's rack (A-frame)

Form : Slanting free style

Method : Here, a form of slanting style is arranged with dried silk grass as first, second and third lines. A few points to be noted in dealing with dried materials are; (1) Dry the fresh flowers you want to use as materials. (2) Dye or color the flowers you have dried. (3) Again dry the dyed or colored materials. When drying the dyed materials, hang them upside down in the shade in a breezy place away from sunlight. (4) Right before using the dried materials, moisten them with water in a spray bottle so that they can be easily bent. An oasis urethan is used instead of pin-holder to insert the materials.

Subordinate : Indian millet and ground cherry are used as subordinates. Cover the ground (base) with mugwort.

Comments : When the harvest season came, Koreans used to carry the harvested crops in this A-frame. Now farmers no longer use this rack because they have tractors.

☐ 추　수

화　재 : 착색 비단풀, 마른 떡갈나무, 수수, 꽈리, 다북쑥

화　기 : 지게

화　형 : 기울이는 자유형

꽂는 법 : 제 1, 2, 3주지를 비단풀로 꽂아 전체적인 선을 잡아 준 뒤에 여러 화재를 조화 있게 꽂는다.

마른 화재는 바람이 잘 통하는 응달에 거꾸로 매달아 말려, 탈색 이나 염색으로 원하는 색을 만들 수 있는 장점이 있다. 침봉 대신에 오아시스나 우레탄을 사용한다.

종지 넣기 : 종지는 주지보다 키를 작게 꽂는다.

각 주지의 사이사이에 철사를 뭉쳐서 넣어 주고, 다북쑥으로 공 간을 메운다.

해　설 : 푸른 가을하늘을 배경으로 풍성한 추수를 한 농부의 지게 를 보는 듯하다. 추수의 계절이 오면 농촌에서는 지게를 사용하였다. 이제는 기계의 발달로 자취를 감춰 가고 있지만 그 향수는 가슴에 남 아 있다.

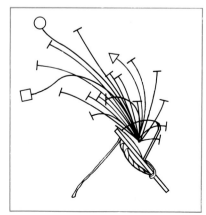

□ **Waiting for You**

Materials : Larch, Dried oak tree branch, Dried lagross, Dried statise, Dried aster

Container : Ki (a Korean winnowing fan)

Form : Slanting free style

Method : Arrange dried pine branch to make first, second and third lines. Fix the first line firmly inside the oasis. The second line is done in a slanting style; the third is in almost a horizontal position, about 180°.

Subordinate : After the lines of the three main branches are made with dry larches, arrange statise and lagross in the center. Bind materials together if they are difficult to insert.

Comments : This winnow called "Ki" is used to clean the grain in Korea. A woman on the farm winnowing seems to be shyly waiting for someone.

□ 기다림

화　재 : 마른 낙엽송, 마른 떡갈나무, 말린 강아지풀, 말린 스타티스, 말린 과꽃

화　기 : 키

화　형 : 기울이는 자유형

꽂는 법 : 제1주지는 말린 낙엽송으로 꽂되 솔방울을 적당히 떼어내어 고정된 우레탄에 꽂는다.

제2주지 역시 선을 살린 낙엽송을 기울여 꽂는다.

제3주지는 낙엽송가지를 거의 눕힌 180° 정도로 꽂는다.

종지 넣기 : 줄기가 가는 화재는 몇 개씩 묶어 꽂는 것이 좋다. 마른 화재 사이에 푸른색으로 착색한 강아지풀을 꽂아 조화를 준다.

해　설 : 곡물을 깨끗이 하기 위해 사용되는 키를 이용한 작품이다. 키질을 하며 먼 산 너머 누군가가 올 것 같아 수줍음 속에 기다리는 여인의 모습을 표현해 보았다.

□ Hunting

Materials : Cattail, Silk grass, Lotus pip, Aster, Tiger osmund, Mugwort
Container : Basket and old root
Form : Upright free style

Method : The cattail first line is arranged high as if one is shooting an arrow. Dried lotus is used as the second line; tiger osmund as the third.
Subordinate : You can use aster and mugwort in a bundle to cover the basket.
Comments : When the horns blow, the hunters run with their arrows. They run through the hills and valleys searching.... Two head pads are decorated to remind us of a typical Korean setting.

□ 사 냥

화 재 : 부들, 비단풀, 연밥, 과꽃, 호랑고비, 다북쑥
화 기 : 소쿠리와 고목 뿌리
화 형 : 바로세우는 자유형

꽃는 법 : 말린 부들을 제 1 주지로 높게 꽃는다.
제 2 주지는 말린 연밥을 곡선이 있는 것으로 꽃는다.
제 3 주지는 역시 말린 호랑고비로 꽃는다.
종지 넣기 : 과꽃과 다북쑥을 뭉치로 꽃아 전체적으로 안정감 있게 꽂는다.
해 설 : 나팔 소리 울리면 사냥군은 활을 메고 뛰어나간다. 언덕과 골짜기를 지나 사냥감을 찾아 뛰고 또 달린다. 2 개의 또아리를 놓아 전통적인 한국적 분위기를 연출해 보았다.

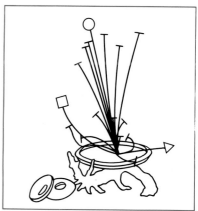

□ South Pacific

Materials : Pampas grass, Bracken, Silk grass, Chinese aster, Statise, Orchid leaf, Patrinia

Container : An old root

Form : Upright free style

Method : In a piece of an old tree, I fixed an oasis with wires and inserted pampas grasses as first line. Colored brackens are the second line. You can curve the stems with your fingers. The third line is asters with patrinia and statise.

Subordinate : Use small flowers as a bunch.

Comments : While traveling through the Pacific I saw many fields of pampas on the seashore. I tried to express the beautiful seashores, and the chorus of shells while I arranged this one.

□ 남태평양 연안

화 재 : 팜파스그래스, 고사리, 비단풀, 과꽃, 난초잎, 스타티스, 마타리

화 기 : 고목 뿌리

화 형 : 바로세우는 자유형

꽂는 법 : 우선 우레탄을 철사로 고목에 고정시킨 다음 꽂는다. 제 1주지는 팜파스그래스를 곧게 꽂아 준다.

제 2주지는 착색한 고사리를 손으로 약간 굽혀 꽂는다.

제 3주지는 과꽃을 뭉치로 하여 꽂는다.

종지 넣기 : 제 1주지를 살려 대응되는 작은 화재를 뭉치로 꽂는다.

해 설 : 남태평양 어느 연안에 무성했던 팜파스밭을 팜파스그래스로 표현해 보았다. 푸른 바다밑 조개들의 밀어가 한창 익어가는 분위기이다.

☐ **The Duchess**

Materials : Peacock tail, Pampas grass, Millet, Statise, Cattail, Bracken, Caladium
Container : An old root
Form : Upright free style

Method : Insert pampas grasses and peacock tail as the first line. Make the second line with caladium. The third line is formed with strong colored brackens.
Subordinate : In the center put small dried materials as a bundle.
Comments : This makes a good decoration for the living room on top of the mantel or in front of the fireplace. You can change the atmosphere by replacing the container with rocks or stones.

①

②

③

☐ 공작부인

화　재 : 공작꼬리, 팜파스그래스, 조, 스타티스, 부들, 고사리, 칼라디움
화　기 : 고목
화　형 : 바로세우는 자유형

꽂는 법 : 팜파스그래스와 공작털로 제 1 주지를 꽂는다.
제 2 주지는 칼라디움으로 꽂는데 줄기 여러 개로 선을 다듬어 꽂는다.
제 3 주지는 고사리로 꽂는다. 고사리는 강한 색으로 입체감을 나타낸다.
종지 넣기 : 중앙 부분은 화재가 주로 작은 것들로 뭉치법으로 꽂는다.
해　설 : 팜파스그래스의 부드러움과 공작털의 화사함을 주는 이 작품은 거실이나 벽난로 장식용으로 좋다. 화기를 바위나 돌 등으로 바꾸면 새로운 분위기를 느낄 수도 있다.

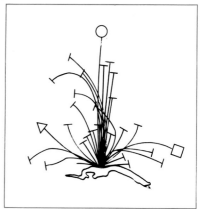

☐ Nocturne

Materials : Peacock tail, Tiger osmund, Lotus pip, Patrinia, Willow branch, Mugwort

    Container : A Korean sieve

    Form : Slanting style

    Method : Fix an oasis in a Korean sieve and bend the stem of peacock tail to form the first, second and third lines.

    Subordinate : Insert willow in between the peacock tail to give a rhythmic feeling. Mugwort and patrinia are used to cover the inner space; lotus shows the contrast between the strong and the weak. Dried tiger osmund covers bottom of the space.

    Comments : Music is flowing. Chopin's Nocturne is spreading and echoing with a beautiful melody through the night air....

①

②

③

☐야상곡

화　재 : 공작꼬리, 호랑고비, 연밥, 마타리, 버들가지, 다북쑥

화　기 : 체

화　형 : 기울이는 형

꽂는 법 : 제 1, 2, 3 주지는 공작털을 구부려 선을 만들어 꽂는다.

종지 넣기 : 우선 버들가지를 다듬어 율동감 있는 모양으로 구부려 공작털 사이에 꽂아 준다. 다북쑥과 마타리는 뭉치로 만들어 안쪽 공간을 메워 주고, 연밥은 강약의 대비를 이루도록 조화 있게 꽂는다. 말린 호랑고비는 아래쪽에 꽂아 전체적으로 안정감을 준다.

해　설 : 음악이 흐른다. 쇼팽의 야상곡이 아름다운 메아리처럼 밤의 적막을 뚫고 화려한 음율이 되어 흐른다.

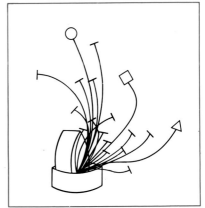

The Origin of Flower Arrangement Form

꽃꽂이 유래
화형

The Origin of Flower Arrangement

Flora, the goddess of flowers, is said to have turned everybody into flowers regardless of whether they practiced virtue or sin.

Back in ancient times, in Egypt and India, two cradles of civilization, people offered flowers as a gift to God, and thus the history of flower arrangement began.

They believed in heavenly gods and offered the flowers to these deities along with other holy offerings.

Flowers were used as expressions of sympathy and tokens of love. From the wall paintings of ancient Egypt, we can see and easily understand this fact.

This wall paintings made in the era of 18th Dynasty of Egypt, shows the widow of the nobleman, offering flowers to console the

꽃꽂이 유래

꽃의 여신인 Flora는 선인이건 악인이건 간에 아름 다운 면이 조금이라도 인정되면 꽃으로 만들었다고 한다.

꽃꽂이의 역사를 고대로 거슬러 올라가 보면 고대 문명의 발상지인 이집트나 인도에서 신에게 바치는 제물로부터 시작되었다고 생각된다.

예를 들면 고대 이집트 사람들은 태양의 신을 믿었 는데 이 태양신께 바치는 제물 중 꽃을 가장 중요시 하여 바쳤다 한다. 또한 이들은 영혼을 위로하기 위 한 수단과, 병자의 위문, 사랑의 표시로 꽃을 사용하 였음을 아래의 고대 이집트 벽화를 통해 볼 수 있다.

이 벽화는 이집트 18왕조 때의 벽화로 귀족의 부인 이 신관들이 최후의 의식을 베풀고 있는 옆에서 미이

Wall painting, 18th Dynasty of Egypt
이집트 18왕조 때의 벽화

soul of her dead husband among the subjects performing the last rites.

Flower arrangement originating from religious ceremonies became varied and systematic in the East and the West in the process of the development of civilization.

In the East, the custom of offering flowers to Buddha (so-called Kongyang-Hwa) was introduced into Korea and Japan from India, the historical Buddhism.

Especially, in India, according to the traditional fact that God does not step on earth as the photograph shows, flowers were strewn flowers at God's feet in the belief that one could be forgiven of sins by so doing. Even today, this custom spread flower during prayer.

The flowers used at that time, were Jassmin, common marigold, and rose.

Flower arrangement in China, we can guess by the bibliography, originated from Kong-

라가 된 남편의 영혼을 달래 주는 모습이다. 그 옆에 몇 개의 화병을 포개어 꽃을 꽂은 모습을 볼 수 있는 데 이는 꽃을 통해 영혼을 위로하였음을 알 수 있다.

꽃꽂이는 인류의 문명 발달 과정에서 동서양을 막론하고 종교 의식이 생기면서부터 그 유형이 다양해지고 체계화되었다.

동양에서는 불교의 발상지인 인도로부터 공양화가 중국을 거쳐 한국과 일본으로 전파되었다고 믿어지며, 이것은 불교의 전파 과정에서 역사적으로 입증되는 것이다.

특히 인도 사람들은 신은 땅을 밟지 않는다는 전통적인 사상으로 사진에서 보는 바와 같이 신의 발 아래 꽃을 뿌림으로써 죄의 사함을 받는다고 믿고 있기 때문에, 지금까지도 신의 발에 꽃을 뿌리고 기도드리는 모습을 볼 수 있다. 이 때 사용된 꽃들은 주로 인도에서 많이 피는 자스민, 금잔화, 장미 등이다.

중국의 꽃꽂이도 불교의 전래로 인한 공양화로부터

Indian pilgrim painting, after 6th century, B.C.
인도의 순례자. 기원전 6세기 이후의 것으로 추정됨

yang-Hwa (the flower offering to Buddha).

In Korea, even before receiving the advent of Buddhism, there are many indications that flowers were used in the ceremonies of Shamanism but the beginning of the full-scale flower arrangement came with Kongyang-Hwa.

In the period of the Shilla Dynasty in the unification of the country when the Buddhism was at its height, the flower offering to the Buddhist Kongyang-Hwa gained importance.

In the Koryo, period after Shilla, when the Buddhism was the state religion, Kongyang-Hwa offerings became the custom and had been used for appreciation. Thus the flower arrangement developed.

Bibliographies including Koryo history, give many indications of Koryo celadon which is world famous for the flower patterns on its surface. The use of celadon as a flower vase indicates our cultural esteem for flowers and

발달하였음을 중국 옛 문헌으로 미루어 짐작이 간다.

한국의 꽃꽂이는 중국에서 불교가 전래되기 전에 무속에서도 꽃을 사용한 흔적을 여러 곳에서 발견할 수 있으나, 본격적인 꽃꽂이는 삼국시대에 불교의 전파로 인해 불전에 연꽃 등을 바치는 공양화를 꽃꽂이의 시초로 보아야 할 것이다. 신라 통일시대에는 불교의 전성기를 맞아 공양화도 꽃꽂이로서 기틀을 마련하게 된다.

불교를 국교로 불교 문화가 절정을 이룬 고려시대에 이르면 공양화의 양식이 체계화되고 나아가서는 감상을 위한 꽃꽂이로 발전해 나감을 보게 된다. 이는 고려사(高麗史) 등 여러 문헌을 통해 알 수 있으며, 세계적으로 널리 알려진 고려 청자에 꽃무늬를 상감한 것으로 미루어 짐작할 수 있다.

또한 이러한 자기가 꽃을 꽂는 병이나 항아리로 널리 사용되었다는 사실을 보더라도 우리 조상의 꽃을 즐기는 수준을 짐작할 수 있으며, 특히 민간에서도

"After-Wedding Celebration," a Korean folk painting
결혼식을 마친 신부가 큰상을 받는 모습을 그린 민화

flower arrangement which was very popular among the common people.

In the Choson period, during which Confucianism overtook Buddhism, we can see many pictures showing various types of pure Korean flower arrangement, which was popular along with tea ceremony and calligraphy in the homes.

In the picture on page 87 showing a bride after the ancient Korean traditional marriage, receiving the dinner on a small table, we see flower arrangements at both ends of the bride's table.

And the four pictures on pages 88 and 89 show the flower arrangements in their systematical forms in the room of a intellectual scholar.

If you observe the first picture carefully, you will notice that even a foliage plant, was used in the flower arrangement, showing variety of flower arrangement materials with emphasis of line.

널리 퍼져 있었음을 알 수 있다.

억불숭유정책을 썼던 조선조에 이르면 민화나 풍속도에서 공양화를 떠난 본격적인 우리 나라의 순수한 꽃꽂이 형태를 엿볼 수 있으며, 다도(茶道), 서도(書道)와 함께 가정에까지 깊숙이 파고 들었음을 알 수 있다.

87페이지의 사진은 결혼식을 마친 신부가 큰상을 받은 모습을 그린 민화인데 신부의 큰상 양쪽에 꽃을 꽂아 놓은 것을 볼 수 있다.

또한 아래의 문방사우 그림 4폭을 보면, 선비 방에 문방사우와 함께 꽃꽂이가 필수적인 것으로 되어 있으며, 한국의 꽃꽂이가 체계화되어 있었음을 알 수 있다.

문방사우 ①을 보면 관엽식물의 잎을 사용하여 한국 꽃꽂이의 특징인 선을 살린 점을 발견할 수 있다. ②는 직립형으로 꽂고 가운데 활짝 핀 꽃을 꽂아 포인트를 주었다. ③은 아래에 넓은 병으로 안정감을

"Four Precious Things of the Study," Korean folk paintings ① ② ③ ④
여러 모양의 문방사우를 그린 민화 ① ② ③ ④

In the Kunson-To (Taoist Immortals), which is the masterpiece of the very famous painter, Mr. Kim, Hong-do, in the latter Choson period there are nymphs wearing flowers in their hair, and carrying flowers on their shoulders, an indication that Koreans adored and enjoyed flowers immensely.

In the picture of Mr. Chang, Sung-op, a most famous artist also in the latter Choson

나타내고, 사군자 중 매화로 공간과 선을 살린 경사형 꽃꽂이이다. ④는 꽃을 뭉치로 꽂고 공간과 선을 살린 한국 꽃꽂이의 전형적인 예인 것 같다.

아울러 이조 후기의 화가 김 홍도의 그림인 군선도는 선녀들의 머리를 꽃으로 장식했으며 꽃을 메고 있

Detail of "Various kinds of things," by Owon Chang Sung-op of Yi Dynasty.

조선조 말기의 화가. 오원 장승업 (1843~1897)의 백물 (百物)

era, we see that the separated style of arrangement of flowers was practiced as early as that time.

Thus Korea has developed its original type of flower arrangement with its ceramic wares since the introduction of Buddhism into this country.

Korea is now making great effort to find its original form of flower arrangement.

Foreigners usually consider the Japanese as the father of Oriental flower arrangement, but it's an undeniable fact that the flower arrangement in Japan originated from Kong-yang-Hwa, the father of flower arrangement in

는 모습을 보면 한국인이 얼마나 꽃을 사랑하고 즐겼는지 알 수 있다.

이조 말기의 화가 장 승업의 그림을 보면 오늘날 한국 꽃꽂이의 형태인 분리형까지 이미 이 때에도 있었음을 알 수 있다.

위에서 고찰한 것과 같이 한국의 꽃꽂이는 불교가 전파되면서부터 도자기의 발전과 함께 독자적인 경지를 구축 발전해왔음을 알 수 있다.

이제 한국의 꽃꽂이도 우리의 고유한 뿌리를 찾는 많은 사람들의 노력으로 차츰 그 모습을 되찾고 있다.

Detail of "Taoist Immortals," by Tanwon Kim Hong-do of Yi Dynasty

조선조 21대 영조 때의 화가. 단원 김홍도(1760~?)의 군선도

"Flowering Plants and Insects," by Shin Saimdang, woman painter of Yi Dynasty. In her paintings, various kinds of present Korean flower arrangement are seen.

조선조 때의 여류 문인, 서화가, 신사임당 (1504~1551) 의 초충도(草蟲圖). 오늘날 한국 꽃꽂이의 여러 형태가 잘 나타나 있다.

Korea which had propagated with Buddhism from India to China, Korea and Japan.

A characteristic of the Korean method of flower arrangement is using a few flowers and twigs without flowers, in order to emphasize the line and space and to express elegance and profound sentiment.

Nowadays, the surrealistic type of flower arrangement is being developed along with the original form of the Korean flower arrangement.

그러나 외국인들은 일본의 꽃꽂이(이께바나)가 동양 꽃꽂이의 시조인 것으로 잘 못 인식하고 있다. 일본의 꽃꽂이가 종교적 의식인 공양화에 기원을 두고 있다면, 일본 꽃꽂이도 불교를 일본에 전한 우리 나라에서 전해진 것임은 의심할 나위가 없다.

우리 나라 꽃꽂이의 특색은 많은 꽃을 사용하지 않고 몇 송이의 꽃을 꽂거나, 꽃 없이 나뭇가지의 선과 공간을 살려 우아하고 깊은 정감을 표현한다고 볼 수 있다. 요즈음엔 고유한 꽃꽂이 형태와 함께 비사실적인 면의 꽃꽂이도 병행하여 발전해 나가고 있다.

right: *Earthen-lamps of Kaya period. They are similar to specific containers which are used at present time.*

오른쪽 : 가야시대의 등잔형 토기. 요즘의 변형 화기와 닮았다. (4 ~ 6 C)

bottom left: *White porcelain vase of Koryo period (mid-12th century)*

bottom right: *Plain white porcelain big jar of Yi Dynasty (17C)*

아래 왼쪽 : 고려시대의 백자 (12C 중반)
아래 오른쪽 : 조선조 때의 백자 항아리 (17C)

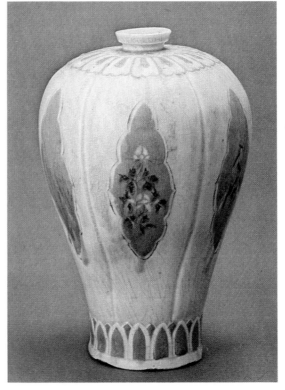

Form (How to Arrange Flower)

BASIC STYLE

In any form, there are three main branches; Chin(Heaven), Yong(Man), In(Earth). The main branch forms the basic style of flower arrangements.

If the main branch is straight up, it is called upright style and slanting style is named when the main branch lay slanted. There is also a subordinated branch which emphasizes main branch and besides three main branches there are subordinated branches. All the subordinated branches usually be smaller than the main branches. However, number of them is not a critical.

● Main Branches

FIRST MAIN BRANCH (the longest line)—◯(Chin)

It is essential elements to make an outline and height.

SECOND MAIN BRANCH (2nd size)—▢(Yong)

It determines, with 3rd branch, width and volume.

THIRD MAIN BRANCH (3rd size)—△(In)

It harmonizes with 1st and 2nd lines.

● Subordinate (T)

It supports and complements the main branches. The volume and numbers are not main considerations.

First subordinate (T)—placed close to the first main branch.

Second subordinate (T)—placed close to the second main branch.

Third subordinate (T)—placed close to the third main branch.

화형

꽃꽂이 기본형

어떤 형에서나 세 가지의 주로 된 선——진(眞), 용(容), 인(仁)——을 가지고 있는데 1주지 즉 주가 되는 가지를 의미하며, 이것은 작품의 형을 이루고 기초가 된다. 주지가 바로 서 있으면 바로세우는 형, 누워(기울어져) 있는 형태이면 기울이는 형으로 된다. 여기에 종지가 있어야하며 주의 종속된 가지이며, 보조역할을 하게 되는 가지를 말한다. 주지 이외에 모든 가지를 종지라 하며, 다소의 관계는 없으나 키가 주지보다 크지 않는 것이 좋다.

●주지

제1주지 (긴 선)◯〈眞〉
작품을 인도하여 전체 움직임을 가짐. 높이에 결정.
제2주지 (두번째 크기)▢〈容〉
인과 더불어 부피와 폭을 결정한다.
제3주지 (세번째 크기)△〈仁〉
◯, ▢을 받들어 조화를 가짐.

●종지 T

도와주는 가지를 말하며, 부피는 상관없으며, 수도 상관이 없다.

◯(진)에 대한 T는 진 가까이 꽂는 것이 좋다.
▢(용)에 대한 T는 용 가까이 꽂는 것이 좋다.
△(인)에 대한 T는 인 가까이 꽂는 것이 좋다.

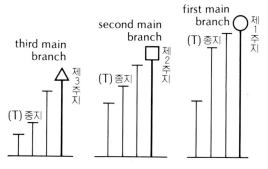

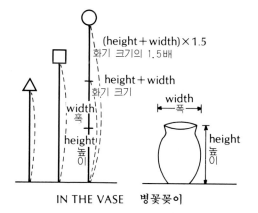

IN THE VASE   병꽃꽂이

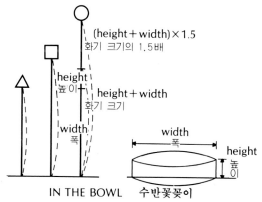

IN THE BOWL   수반꽃꽂이

93

● Length of the branches

First branch (O)

Small size—Height of the container plus its diameter (width) (H + W)

Medium size—One and half of the small size (S + S/2)

Large size— Twice the small size (2 × S)

The third size (long size) is used more often than the other two.

● 길이

진의 길이 { 소—그릇의 폭+높이 / 중—小+$\frac{小}{2}$ / 대—小×2

이 셋 중 하나를 선택하며 대개는 대(大)를 택한다.

HEIGHT OF FIRST MAIN BRANCH
O 의 높이

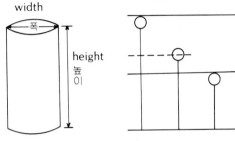

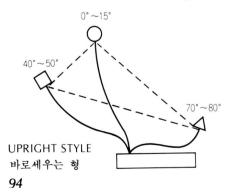

width 폭 height 높이

Second branch (□): ¾ of the first branch in most cases, but sometimes ½ or ⅓ of the first branch.

Third branch (△): ¾ of the second branch, but sometimes ½ or ⅓ of the second branch.

용의 길이 ○의 길이에 비례하여 결정된다.

선택한 진의 $\frac{3}{4}$, $\frac{1}{2}$, $\frac{1}{3}$ 을 택한다.

대개는 $\frac{3}{4}$ 을 택하나 크고 탐스러운 경우 ○의 $\frac{1}{2}$, $\frac{1}{3}$ 을 잡는다. 같은 가지는 $\frac{3}{4}$ 으로 정한다.

인의 길이 □의 길이에 비례하며, 선택된 용의 $\frac{3}{4}$, $\frac{1}{2}$, $\frac{1}{3}$ 을 정한다.

● Angle

First line 0°—15° from all directions.

Second line 40°—50° with the left front.

Third line 70°—80° with the right front.

● 각도

○은 전후좌우 0°~15°

□은 수직선상의 40°~50°

△은 수직선상의 70°~80°

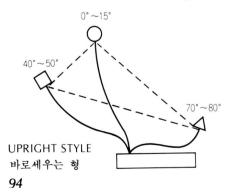

UPRIGHT STYLE
바로세우는 형

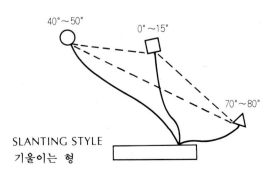

SLANTING STYLE
기울이는 형

● Face of flowers
Generally flower faces look at each other.

face to face
마주 본 경우

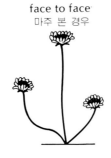

● 꽃의 얼굴
꽃의 얼굴은 서로 마주보는 것이좋다.
때로는 어긋나게도 꽂는 경우가 있다.

opposite
어긋난 경우

Small flowers may be arranged face to face but large flowers such sun-flowers and calla lilies should be placed facing opposite directions.

꽃송이가 작은 꽃일 때는 서로
얼굴을 마주보게 꽂는 것이 좋으
나, 해바라기나 칼라 같이 꽃송
이가 큰 꽃은 서로 어긋나도록
꽂는 것이 훨씬 좋다.

● Pin-holder's location
Pin-holder is placed with consideration of size of container (or box) which contains the holders. In practice, the holders are placed in corner. This pin-holder may be placed in the left or right end of the container separated from the first one with proportion of 7:3.

● 침봉의 위치
침봉상에서 공간을 생각하게 되므로 한쪽으로 치우
쳐 놓는다. 10으로 잡으면 7 : 3의 위치에다 침봉을
놓는다.

Place at one of the four sides.
화기의 좌우에 혹은 앞뒤쪽에
놓는다. (1, 2, 3, 4)

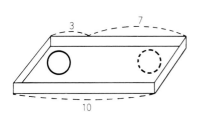

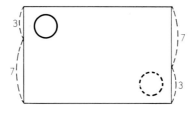

ROUND CONTAINER
둥근 형일 때

SQUARE CONTAINER 화기가 사각인 경우

● Space and line
Space and line must be harmonized. Two basic practices (See the picture) are recommended for this harmony.

● 공간과 선
공간과 선을 살리기 위해 바른 모양과 반대 모양을
연습한다.

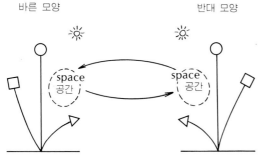

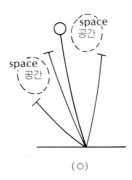

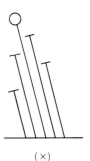

Insert the branch toward the sun. 해를 향하여 꽃는다

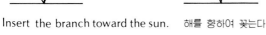

VARIATION OF FORM

화형의 종류

● Basic Upright Style

● 바로세우는 형

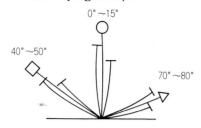
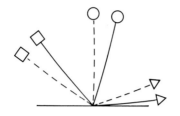
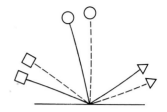

● Basic Slanting Style

● 기울이는 기초형

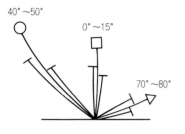
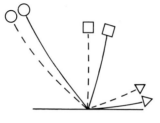
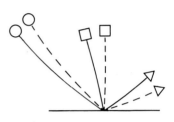

● Variation No. 1 Upright

● 바로세우는 1응용

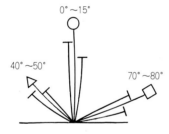
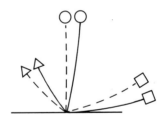
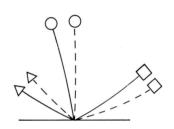

● Variation No. 1 Slanting

● 기울이는 1응용

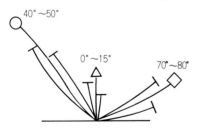
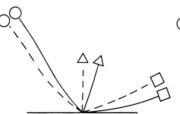
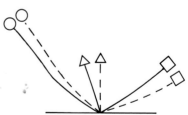

● Variation No. 2 Upright

● 바로세우는 2응용

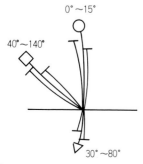
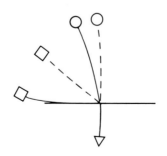
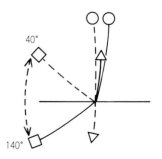

- **Variation No. 2 Slanting**　　　●기울이는 2응용

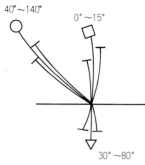

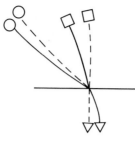

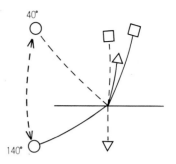

- **Variation No.3 Upright**　　　●바로세우는 3응용

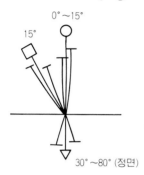

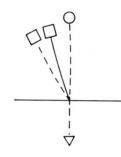

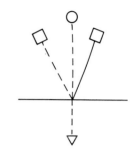

- **Variation No. 3 Slanting**　　　●기울이는 3응용

여러 가지 응용을 할 수 있다.

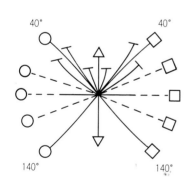

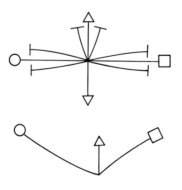

- **Variation No. 4 Upright**　　　●바로세우는 4응용

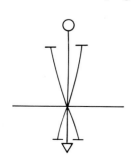

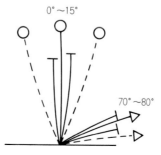

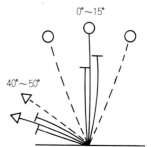

□ can be omissable.　　□이 생략된다

97

● **Variation No. 4 Slanting**

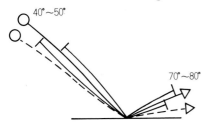

●기울이는 4응용

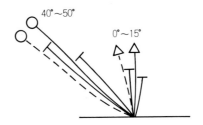

● **Variation No. 5 Upright**

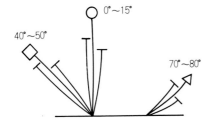

●바로세우는 5응용

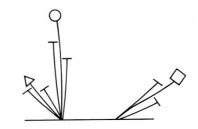

● **Variation No. 5 Slanting**

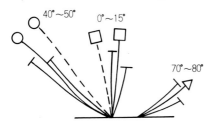

●기울이는 5응용

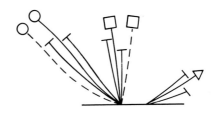

● **Variation No. 6 Upright**

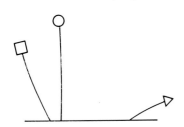

●바로세우는 6응용

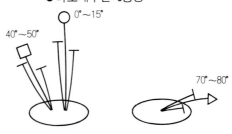

● **Variation No. 6 Slanting**

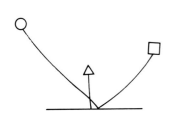

●기울이는 6응용

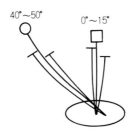

● **The Other Styles**
  All direction style
  Free style

●기타
  사방화
  자유화형

Basic Method

BASIC UPRIGHT STYLE

Materials : Ixia, Chrysanthemum
Container : Celadon bowl
Treatment : Ixia—Cut in water. Chrysanthemum—Treating with salt water or burning the cut tip.

Method : The length of the flowers must be proportional to the container. The first line should be erected toward the back of the pinholder so that the line can be put slanting within a range of 0° to 15° from the vertical.

The second line should be cut to a length of three-quarters of the first line and erected to form a 40° to 50° angle with line No. 1. The third line should be between one-third and one-half of line No. 2 and erected so as to form a 70° to 80° angle from the first line.

Supporting branches can be used, and may vary in number but the heights of the supporting branches should always be lower than the main line.

기초 꽃꽂이 실제

바로세우는 형

화 재 : 익시아, 국화
화 기 : 청자 수반
처 리 법 : 익시아 — 물속자르기
국화 — 염열탕, 줄기끝 태우기

꽃는 법 : 제 1주지의 길이를 정하여 자른다. 보통은 그릇 폭에 그릇의 높이를 더하여 길이를 정하는데 여기에서는 그릇의 폭과 높이를 더한 것에 2배를 해서 잘라 꽂는다. 1주지는 0°에서 15°로 곧게 꽂는다.

제 2주지는 1주지를 중심으로 45°~50° 기울여 꽂고, 높이는 1주지의 3/4 정도로 잘라 꽂는다.

제 3주지는 1주지를 중심으로 70°~80°가 되게 꽂되 길이는 2주지의 3/4 이나 1/2 이 되도록 꽂는다. 주지의 부피가 클 때에는 1/3 이 되게 꽂을 수도 있다.

종지를 꽂을 때에는 길이가 각 주지보다 작아야 하지만 수는 상관치 않아도 좋다.

좀더 필요한 꽃이나 나무로 보충을 하여 작품을 완성시킨다.

BASIC SLANTING STYLE

Materials : Spiraea thunbergii, Rose
Container : Water basin (modern)
Treatment : Spiraea thunbergii—No treatment necessary. Rose—Burning the cut tip of stem or boiling in salt water.

Method : The main line is arranged at 40° to 50°. The second line is erected at 0° to 15° The third line is arranged to the right at 70° to 80°.

(1) The form is a triangle, the same as in the basic upright style. The main line is slanted a little, and the second line is slanted 15° at the left side.

(2) The supporting branches should be arranged in such a way that it looks as though they are coming from the same root but not too close to the main branch.

(3) When using roses, the length should not be too long. If too long, the arrangement would appear unstable. The flowers should face forward. Plant leaves can be used to support the flowers and to cover the pin-holder. There should be ample space between the second and third branches.

기울이는 기초형

　화 재 : 설유화, 장미
　화 기 : 현대 작품
　처 리 법 : 설유화 – 처리 불필요
　　　　　　장미 – 줄기끝 태우기, 염열탕
　꽂는 법 : 제 1 주지는 침봉과 수직선에서 40° ～ 50° 정도 뉘여서 꽂는다.
　제 2 주지는 수직선에서 0° ～15° 가 되도록 꽂되 경사형일 경우에는 10° ～15° 기울여 꽂는다.
　제 3 주지는 수직선에서 70° ～80° 기울여 오른쪽으로 꽂는다.
　(1) 길이는 직립형과 마찬가지로 정하고, 구성도 역시 삼각형이 되도록 한다. 제 1 주지는 15° 기울여 꽂고, 제 2 주지도 따라서 기울이게 꽂는다.
　(2) 종지는 나뭇가지 위쪽은 떨어지게 꽂고 밑쪽은 붙여 꽂아 한나무에서 갈라져 나온 것처럼 보이게 한다.
　(3) 장미는 약간 짧게 잘라 안정감이 있도록 꽂고, 방향은 앞을 향하여 어우러지게 꽂는다. 침봉을 가려 주기 위해 푸른 나뭇잎을 사용하여 꽃받침용으로도 썼다. 이 꽃꽂이는 제 2 주지와 3 주지 사이에 공간을 넉넉히 주었다.

UPRIGHT SEPARATE STYLE

Materials : Flowering quince, Pekinensis (brassica campestris), Calla lily

Container : An oval-shaped, black water basin.

Treatment : Flowering quince—No treatment required. Calla lily—Cut in water, inserting wire in the stem. Cabbage flower (pekinensis) —Cut in water.

Method : This is a basic upright form separated or slanted to emphasize the beauty of space.

(1) First of all, insert the first line at an angle of 15°, the second line at about 45°, using a small pin-holder. The degree and shape of the arrangement can be changed as desired.

(2) Calla lily is used as the third line in place of a tree branch. The subordinates of first and second main lines can also be tree branches. The angle of the third branch is 0° to 15°

(3) Flowers are used for the first, second and the third lines here. Pekinensis is used at the base and to cover the pin-holder. If the empty space seems too great, stones or an old tree bark can be added.

분리형

화 재 : 산당화, 유채화, 칼라
화 기 : 타원형 검은 수반
처 리 법 : 산당화 — 처리 불필요
　　　　유채화 — 물속자르기
　　　　칼라 — 물속자르기 (줄기 속에 철사 넣기)
꽂는 법 : 이 형은 기초형의 직립형이나 기울이는 형을 분리시켜 꽂는 것으로 공간을 더욱 아름답게 강조시키는 꽃꽂이다. 작은 침봉 2개를 사용한다.

제1주지는 왼쪽 침봉에 15°쯤 기울여 왼쪽으로 꽂는다.

제2주지는 오른쪽 침봉에 45°쯤 기울여 꽂는다. 꽂는 사람에 따라 각자의 개성을 살려 각도나 모양은 얼마든지 응용하여도 된다.

제3주지는 왼쪽 침봉에 거의 똑바로 세워 1주지와 2주지 사이에 엇비슷이 꽂는다. 1, 2주지가 나무인 것에 대해 3주지는 꽃을 꽂음으로 부드러움을 주었다.

제1, 2주지의 보조로는 1, 2주지보다 작은 나뭇가지로 꽂고, 제1, 2, 3의 종지는 꽃으로 꽂아 주고 유채화로 밑받침을 하여 침봉도 가려 준다.

완성된 작품의 공간이 너무 허전한 느낌이 들 경우에는 밑에 돌을 깔거나 작은 고목을 곁들여 장식해도 좋다.

ARRANGING FLOWERS IN A VASE

Materials : Prunus persica(peach), snapdragon.

Container : Round–shaped vase

Treatment : Peach—None required. Snapdragon—Cut in water, dip in alcohol.

Arranging flowers in a vase is much more difficult than it appears. Beginners to arrange flowers in the vase first, not knowing how hard it is.

Method : First, the length of the first line should be decided, that is, twice the length of the vase plus its width. The mouth of the vase is covered by using subordinate stems fixed in various ways. Here the cross method is used to support the branches.

When this method is not possible, bind the supporting stems directly and firmly to the branches. After the main branch is fixed firmly, we proceed to the next step of inserting the second branch. If the second branch does not stay firmly, again use the supporting twigs; then finish the arrangement by inserting the flowers between the tree branches. Flower stems can be bent a little to fix their position.

병꽃꽂이

화 재 : 복숭아나무, 금어초

화 기 : 청원통병

처리 법 : 복숭아 – 처리 불필요
　　　　금어초 – 물속자르기, 알코올에 담근다.

꽂는 법 : 제 1 주지는 복숭아나무로 병의 폭과 높이를 더하여 2 배한 길이로 잘라, +자로 묶은 보조 가지를 이용하여 튕기는 방법으로 꽂았다. 1 주지가 절대로 움직이지 않도록 특히 주의해야만 한다.

제 2 주지 역시 복숭아나무를 1 주지 길이의 3 / 4 으로 하여 잘라 꽂는다.

제 3 주지는 금어초로 2 주지의 3 / 4 이나 1 / 2 로 길이를 정하여 자르고 가지를 약간 구부려 꽂는다.

제 1, 2 주지의 종지는 1, 2 주지를 중심으로 복숭아나무를 꽂고, 제 3 주지의 종지는 금어초로 꽂아 완성시킨다.

수반꽂꽂이와 마찬가지로 병꽃꽂이도 모든 형을 이용하여 꽂을 수가 있다.

꽃 한 송이를 꽂아도 그 꽃의 크기와 모양, 그 꽃을 꽂을 병의 모습을 잘 이용하여 꽂는 것이 꽃꽂이의 기본이라 하겠다.

When inserting flowers as subordinate to the first, second and third lines, the flowers and leaves which are under water should be removed. As they soon decay and make the water stale.

In the four corners of the mouth of the vase, one corner is usually left open, to let the air into the vase to prevent fast decaying. Flower arrangements in a vase show the beauty of line and space.

병꽃꽂이 할 때 주의할 점은 화기 한 구석을 비워 신선한 공기가 들어갈 수 있도록 하며 화재의 잎이나 봉오리가 잠기지 않도록 한다. 이것은 물이 부패 되는 것을 막으며 꽃의 수명과 관계된다.

Arranging Flowers in a Tall Vase

Different from arranging in a bowl or a flat container, one does not have a pin-holder in which to insert the materials; thus, it is more difficult to fix the materials. Generally the following methods are used when arranging in a tall vase.

1. Subordinate branches

This method is the most frequently used. Thick and heavy branches are difficult to balance because they are curved. Use subordinate branches at the bottom of the vase to support the main branch. One of the subordinate branches should touch the top rim of the vase and the other reach the bottom of the vase for support.

2. Cross method

Use branches crisscrossing at the top of the vase to keep the materials fixed. The methods of crisscrossing are various. The most popular is in the form of a "+" or an "X". Other methods used are −, =, T, Y, V, and #. Pebbles, sand and empty cans also may be placed at the base.

병꽃꽂이의 요령

병꽃꽂이는 수반꽃꽂이와는 달리 침봉을 사용하지 않으므로 화재를 마음대로 고정시키기 어려운 점이 있다. 병꽃꽂이는 다음과 같은 방법을 이용하여 화재를 고정시켜 꽃꽂이를 한다.

1. 보충 가지를 이용한다

병꽃꽂이에 가장 많이 사용하는 방법으로 보충 가지를 이용하여 화재를 고정시키는 것이다.

굵고 무거우며 굴곡이 심한 화재는 균형이 잘 잡히지 않아 엉뚱한 방향으로 기울어지기 십상이다. 이때 화기 밑바닥에 닿을 탄력 있는 보충가지를 준비하여 윗부분을 조금 쪼개고, 화재의 밑동을 약간 쪼개어 서로 엇갈리게 끼워 병 속에 꽂는다.

주의할 점은 화재의 나뭇가지는 병 주둥이와 안벽에, 보충 가지는 병 밑바닥에 닿아 완전히 고정시켜야 한다.

2. 칸지르기

화기인 병 주둥이 약간 밑에 나뭇가지를 이용하여 칸을 질러 화재를 지탱하여 고정시키는 방법이다.

화재의 분량과 성질에 따라 여러 형태의 칸지르기 방법이 있으나 +자형, ×자형이 가장 많이 사용되고 있다. 그 밖에 칸지르기 방법에는 ─자형, ＝자형, T자형, Y자형, V자형, #자형 등이 있으며, 병 속에 자갈, 모래, 빈통 등을 넣고 한다.

Fix the branch at the rim of the vase
병 벽에 완전히 닿도록 꽂는다

Fix each end of the branches crosswise
끝을 서로 엇갈리게 끼워 꽂는다

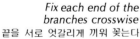

Bind and fix the branch with subordinate branch
보충가지와 묶어 고정시킨다

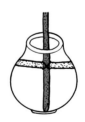

+ type cross method
+자형 칸지르기

− type cross method
─자형 칸지르기

● **Flower preservation methods**

● 간단한 꽃 처리법

Under-water cutting
물속자르기

Burning the cut tip
줄기끝태우기

Boiling in salt water
염열탕

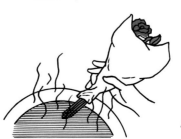

Dipping in alcohol
알코올에 담그기

107

AUTHOR'S RECENT ACTIVITIES

저자의 활동 모습

*The author, instructing flower arrangement to a ladies'
group at the Eighth Army, Yongsan.*

매주 2회 미 8군내에서 꽃꽂이를 지도하는 저자와 회원들.

The author, disseminating the finer points of kkokkoji.

외국인들을 지도하고 있는 저자.

Flower exhibition celebrating America's Independence Day.

매년 열리는 미국 독립일을 기념하는 꽃꽂이 전시회.

Flower arrangement demonstration, held at the Chrystal Ball Room of the Lotte Hotel.

롯데 크리스탈 룸에서 열렸던 강습회. 대성황을 이루었다.

외국인을 위한 강습회를 마치고 관심 있는 많은 외국인들에게 개인적으로 설명을 하고 있다.

The author, giving individual lessons.

The author winning the Cultural Education Award, sponsored by International Cultural Association in December, 1983.

1983년 12월, 국제 문화 협회에서 수상한 문화 교육상을 받음.

The author, posing with Mr. May, chief of Moyer and Craft Center and guest members, after a flower exhibition celebrating America's Independence.

미국 독립 기념 전시회를 마치고 외국인 회원들과 함께 Moyer and Craft Center 책임자인 Mr. May를 모시고.

The author at the flower exhibition celebrating the 22nd anniversary of the founding of MBC, 1983.

M.B.C 22주년 창사 기념 꽃꽂이 전시회 때의 저자.